The Complete Book of Spanish

Thinking Kids™
Carson Dellosa Education
Greensboro, North Carolina

Thinking Kids™
Carson Dellosa Education
P.O. Box 35665
Greensboro, NC 27425 USA

Printed in the USA • All rights reserved.   ISBN 978-1-4838-2686-8
10-115201151

Table of Contents

My Spanish Book

Me llamo _____

Nombre_____

Numbers

uno

dos

tres

cuatro

cinco

Numbers

seis

siete

nueve

diez

ocho

Nombre_____

Numbers 1–5

Say each word out loud.

uno		1
dos	 	2
tres	  	3
cuatro	   	4
cinco	    	5

Nombre_____

Number Review

Write the number next to the Spanish word. Circle the correct number of animals for each number shown. Then, color the pictures.

uno ▢

cinco ▢

dos ▢

cuatro ▢

tres ▢

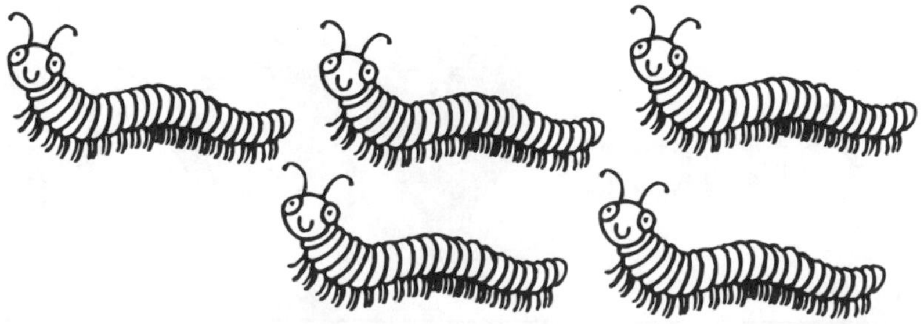

Nombre_____

Matching Numbers

Draw a line from the word to the correct picture. Then, color the pictures.

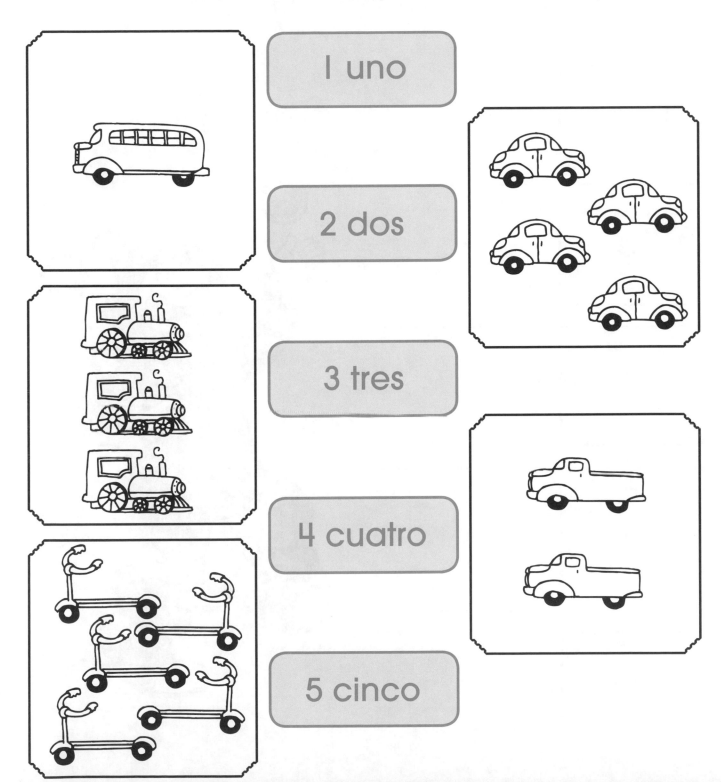

1 uno

2 dos

3 tres

4 cuatro

5 cinco

Number the Stars

Draw the correct number of stars next to each number.

uno

_____

dos

_____

tres

_____

cuatro

_____

cinco

Nombre_____

Numbers 1-5 Matching

Draw a line to match each object to the number that is written in Spanish.

uno   1

dos   2

tres   3

cuatro 4

cinco   5

Nombre_____

Numbers 6–10 Matching

Draw a line to match each object to the number that is written in Spanish.

seis   6

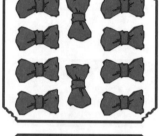

siete   7

ocho   8

nueve   9

diez   10

Nombre_____

Count the Cookies

In each box at the left, write the number that matches the Spanish word. Cross out the correct number of cookies to show the number written in Spanish. The first one is done for you.

| 2 | dos | 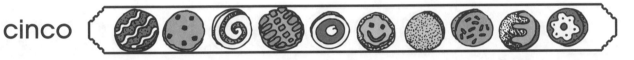 |

| | cinco |  |

| | ocho | |

| | siete |  |

| | cuatro |  |

Nombre_____

Count the Cookies

In each box at the left, write the number that matches the Spanish word. Cross out the correct number of cookies to show the number written in Spanish.

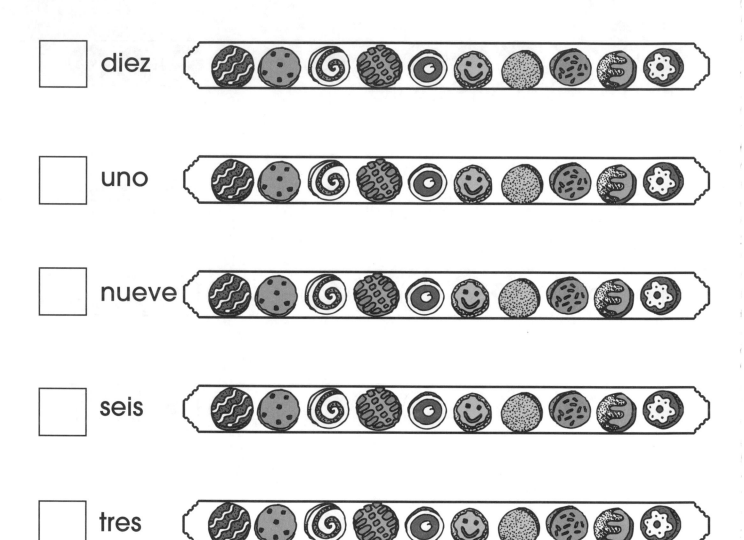

diez

uno

nueve

seis

tres

Nombre_____

My Favorite Number

Write your favorite number from 1 to 10 in the boxes. Draw a picture to show that number.

My favorite number is [   ].

In Spanish it is called [   ].

Nombre_____

Circles 1-10

Draw the correct number of circles in each box.

uno		seis	
dos		siete	
tres		ocho	
cuatro		nueve	
cinco		diez	

Nombre_____

Coloring 0–10

Color or circle the number of butterflies that shows the number written in Spanish.

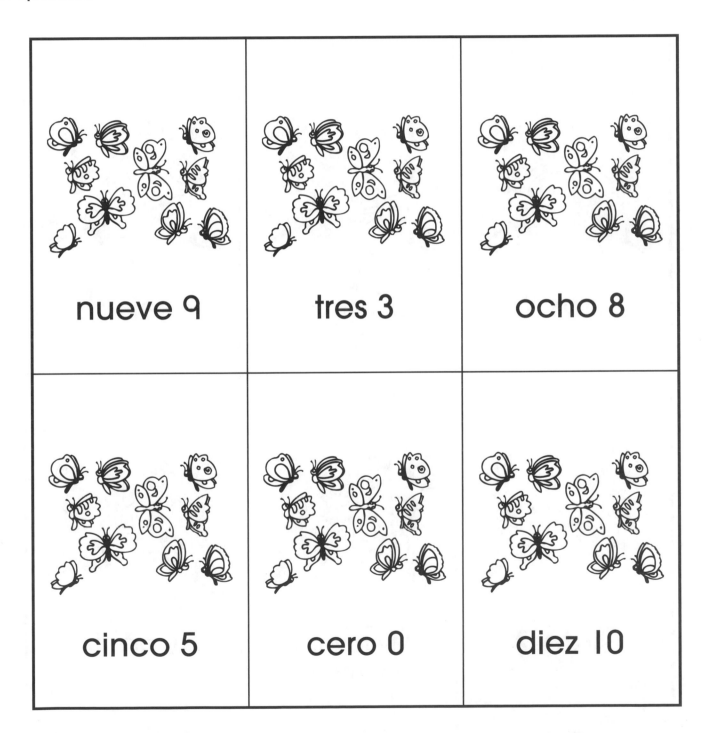

| nueve 9 | tres 3 | ocho 8 |
| cinco 5 | cero 0 | diez 10 |

Nombre_____

Coloring 0-10

Color or circle the number of butterflies that shows the number written in Spanish.

Nombre_____

Numbers 0-10

Trace and write each of the number words from 0 to 10 in Spanish.
Use the words at the left to help you.

0   cero   cero

1   uno   uno

2   dos   dos

3   tres   tres

4   cuatro cuatro

5   cinco   cinco

6   seis   seis

7   siete   siete

8   ocho   ocho

9   nueve   nueve

10 diez   diez

Numbers 0-10

Say each word out loud. Circle the number that tells the meaning of the word.

seis	5	0	6
ocho	1	9	8
uno	3	1	8
cero	8	10	0
siete	9	7	1
tres	0	3	5
diez	10	8	7
nueve	4	2	9
cuatro	7	5	4
dos	2	6	3
cinco	6	4	5

Nombre_____

Dot-to-Dot

Connect the dots. Start with the Spanish word for one and stop at ten.
What shape did you get? _____

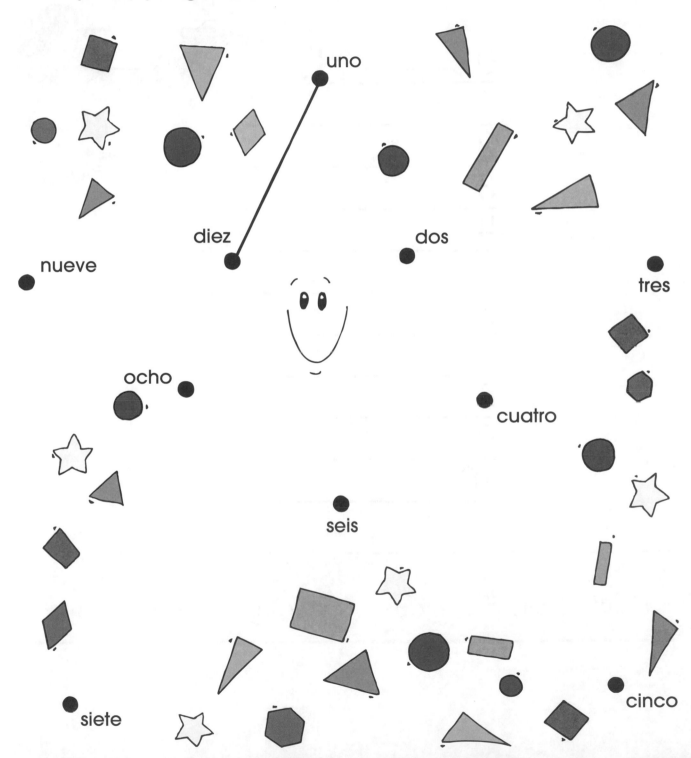

Nombre_____

Numbers 0–20

Write the number words from 0 to 10 in Spanish. Use the words in the box below to help you. An example is done for you.

0 **cero** _____

1 _____

2 _____

3 _____

4 _____

5 _____

6 _____

7 _____

8 _____

9 _____

10 _____

siete	ocho	uno	seis	nueve
cero	cinco	dos	cuatro	diez	tres

Nombre_____

Numbers 0–20

Write the numbers beside each Spanish word. An example is done for you.

_____11_____ once

_____ doce

_____ trece

_____ catorce

_____ quince

_____ dieciséis

_____ diecisiete

_____ dieciocho

_____ diecinueve

_____ veinte

Now, count from 1 to 20 in Spanish. Point to the numbers as you say them.

1	2	3	4	5	6	7	8	9	10
11	12	13	14	15	16	17	18	19	20

Show Your Numbers

In each box, write the number for the word written.
Then, draw and color pictures that show the numbers.

dieciséis means

trece means

catorce means

seis means

once means

ocho means

Nombre_____

Show Your Numbers

In each box, write the number for the word written.
Then, draw and color pictures that show the numbers.

dos means

veinte means

doce means

diez means

quince means

cinco means

Nombre_____

Numbers Illustration

Write the number. Draw that many things in the box. The first one is done for you.

☆☆☆☆ ☆☆☆☆ **ocho** means __8__	**cinco** means _____	**diecisiete** means _____
doce means _____	**uno** means _____	**dos** means _____

Nombre_____

Numbers Illustration

Write the number. Draw that many things in the box.

catorce means _____	**nueve** means _____	**veinte** means _____
siete means _____	**cuatro** means _____	**quince** means _____

Nombre_____

Number Puzzle

Write the English number words in the puzzle spaces. Follow the Spanish clues.

Word Bank

one	nine	fourteen
two	ten	seventeen
six	eleven	eighteen
eight	thirteen	twenty

DOWN
1. diecisiete
2. veinte
4. uno
8. nueve
9. dieciocho
10. diez

ACROSS
1. seis
3. ocho
5. catorce
6. trece
7. once
10. dos

Nombre_____

Counting On

Follow a pattern to write the numbers from 21–29. Change *veinte* (20) to *veinti* and add the number words from *uno* to *nueve*. (Watch for accent marks on *dos*, *tres*, and *seis*.)

Rewrite the number words in the Word Bank in order.

Word Bank

veintiséis	veintisiete	veintitrés
veintidós	treinta	veintiocho
veinticinco	veintinueve	veinticuatro
veintiuno		

21 _____   26 _____

22 _____   27 _____

23 _____   28 _____

24 _____   29 _____

25 _____   30 _____

Complete the pattern to write the numbers from 31–39. Use the word *y* to join *treinta* (30) with the number words *uno* to *nueve*.

30 _____   35 _____

31 _____   36 _____

32 _____   37 _____

33 _____   38 _____

34 _____   39 _____

Number Find

Circle the Spanish number words that you find in the word search. Then, write the English meaning of each word.

d	u	e	t	e	i	s	o	d	n	e	e
t	o	a	i	z	l	h	i	u	c	v	t
r	v	c	t	j	c	e	e	a	h	l	e
e	j	e	e	o	c	v	t	u	i	h	i
s	t	p	i	i	e	o	g	n	e	e	s
b	i	r	o	n	r	v	p	q	m	c	i
z	t	c	e	c	t	m	t	c	s	n	t
e	h	a	e	i	c	i	v	h	o	i	n
o	v	p	z	s	n	i	d	e	d	u	i
e	t	n	i	e	v	t	n	ó	c	q	e
s	e	i	s	a	z	o	a	c	s	n	v
v	e	i	n	t	i	u	n	o	o	c	o

Spanish Word	English	Spanish Word	English
doce	_____	treinta	_____
catorce	_____	siete	_____
veintiuno	_____	ocho	_____
veintisiete	_____	veintidós	_____
once	_____	cinco	_____
dos	_____	seis	_____
nueve	_____	quince	_____
veinte	_____	tres	_____
		dieciocho	_____

Nombre_____

Counting by Tens

The Spanish numbers ten, twenty, thirty, forty, and fifty are written out of order below. Write the value of each number word in the blank.

____ treinta   ____ cincuenta   ____ cuarenta

____ diez   ____ veinte

Write the numbers from 30–59 in Spanish.

30	_____	45	_____
31	_____	46	_____
32	_____	47	_____
33	_____	48	_____
34	_____	49	_____
35	_____	50	_____
36	_____	51	_____
37	_____	52	_____
38	_____	53	_____
39	_____	54	_____
40	_____	55	_____
41	_____	56	_____
42	_____	57	_____
43	_____	58	_____
44	_____	59	_____

Number Search

Circle the Spanish number words that you find in the word search. Write the English meanings at the bottom of the page next to the Spanish words from the puzzle.

c	s	c	r	i	w	d	v	k	z	r	e	t
r	i	y	e	u	g	m	l	e	k	v	r	k
e	i	n	i	r	y	q	i	q	e	e	s	g
o	y	p	c	a	o	d	c	u	c	i	y	p
d	y	t	f	o	t	u	n	e	e	y	i	d
r	l	z	i	w	a	n	e	s	o	t	c	o
s	r	q	o	r	c	v	e	c	e	n	w	n
o	g	h	e	u	e	z	s	u	n	c	c	u
d	c	n	a	i	a	j	r	i	c	i	o	e
o	t	t	n	r	n	k	x	s	e	n	u	d
a	r	t	q	u	i	n	c	e	e	t	i	q
o	e	b	a	t	n	i	e	r	t	r	e	c
c	a	t	o	r	c	e	u	e	e	d	t	h

Spanish Word	English	Spanish Word	English
cero	_____	dos	_____
cuatro	_____	seis	_____
ocho	_____	diez	_____
doce	_____	catorce	_____
veinte	_____	cuarenta	_____
uno	_____	tres	_____
cinco	_____	siete	_____
nueve	_____	once	_____
trece	_____	quince	_____
treinta	_____	cincuenta	_____

Nombre_____

Spanish Alphabet

EL ABECEDARIO (EL ALFABETO) EN ESPAÑOL

Aa	a	Jj	jota	Rr	ere
Bb	be	Kk	ka	Ss	ese
Cc	ce	Ll	ele	Tt	te
Dd	de	Mm	eme	Uu	u
Ee	e	Nn	ene	Vv	ve
Ff	efe	Ññ	eñe	Ww	doble u
Gg	ge	Oo	o	Xx	equis
Hh	hache	Pp	pe	Yy	i griega
Ii	i	Qq	cu	Zz	zeta

Rhyming Vowel Practice

Say these sentences out loud:

A, E, I, O U, ¡Más sabe el burro que tú!

A, E, I, O, U, ¿Cuántos años tienes tú?

Nombre_____

Listening Practice

Say the Spanish word for each number out loud.
Write the first letter of the words you hear.

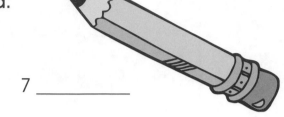

1 _____   4 _____   7 _____

2 _____   5 _____   8 _____

3 _____   6 _____   9 _____

Color the letters of the Spanish alphabet. Say them in Spanish as you color them.

A B C D E F G

H I J K L M N

Ñ O P Q R S T

U V W X Y Z

Nombre_____

The Alphabet

El abecedario (the alphabet)

a	a	**h**	hache	**ñ**	eñe	**u**	u
b	be	**i**	i	**o**	o	**v**	ve
c	ce	**j**	jota	**p**	pe	**w**	doble u
d	de	**k**	ka	**q**	cu	**x**	equis
e	e	**l**	ele	**r**	ere	**y**	i griega
f	efe	**m**	eme	**s**	ese	**z**	zeta
g	ge	**n**	ene	**t**	te		

Listening Practice

Write each letter of the alphabet as you say it out loud.

1. _____   7. _____   13. _____   19. _____   25. _____

2. _____   8. _____   14. _____   20. _____   26. _____

3. _____   9. _____   15. _____   21. _____   27. _____

4. _____   10. _____   16. _____   22. _____

5. _____   11. _____   17. _____   23. _____

6. _____   12. _____   18. _____   24. _____

Nombre_____

The Alphabet

El abecedario (the alphabet)

a	a	**j**	jota	**r**	ere
b	be	**k**	ka	**s**	ese
c	ce	**l**	ele	**t**	te
d	de	**m**	eme	**u**	u
e	e	**n**	ene	**v**	ve
f	efe	**ñ**	eñe	**w**	doble u
g	ge	**o**	o	**x**	equis
h	hache	**p**	pe	**y**	i griega
i	i	**q**	cu	**z**	zeta

Listening Practice

Write the Spanish word for each number below. Then, spell each word out loud.

1 _____   5 _____   9 _____   13 _____

2 _____   6 _____   10 _____   14 _____

3 _____   7 _____   11 _____   15 _____

4 _____   8 _____   12 _____   16 _____

Nombre_____

Parts of Speech

you

tú

you

usted

pretty

bonita

ugly

feo

Nombre_____

Parts of Speech

happy

feliz

to read

leer

sad

triste

to play

jugar

to eat

comer

Using You

Spanish uses two different forms of the pronoun **you**.

Tú is used when talking to

1. someone you refer to by a first name.
2. your sister, brother, or cousin.
3. a classmate.
4. a close friend.
5. a child younger than yourself.

Usted (Ud.) is used when talking to

1. someone with a title.
2. an older person.
3. a stranger.
4. a person of authority.

Write the names of 6 or more people in each box below.

Use **tú** when you are talking to . . .	Use **usted** when you are talking to . . .

Nombre_____

Picking Pronouns

Spanish uses two different forms of the pronoun *you*.

Tú is used when talking to

1. someone you refer to by a first name.
2. your sister, brother, or cousin.
3. a classmate.
4. a close friend.
5. a child younger than yourself.

usted

Usted (Ud.) is used when talking to

1. someone with a title.
2. an older person.
3. a stranger.
4. a person of authority.

Explain to whom you might be talking and what you are asking in each question.

¿Cómo te llamas tú? _____

¿Cómo se llama usted? _____

¿Cómo estás tú? _____

¿Cómo está usted? _____

¿Cuántos años tienes tú?_____

¿Cuántos años tiene usted? _____

Nombre_____

Who Is It?

Write the names of people you may know that fit each description below.

tú-informal or familiar form of you	
someone you refer to by first name	
your sister or brother (or cousin)	
a classmate	
a close friend	
a child younger than yourself	

usted-formal or polite form of you	
someone with a title	
an older person	
a stranger	
a person of authority	

How would you speak to each person below? Write *tú* or *usted* after each person named.

1. Dr. Hackett_____
2. Susana_____
3. a four-year-old_____
4. your grandfather_____
5. the governor_____

6. your best friend_____
7. your sister_____
8. the principal_____
9. a classmate _____
10. a stranger _____

Nombre_____

Masculine and Feminine

All Spanish nouns and adjectives have gender. This means they are either masculine or feminine. Here are two basic rules to help determine the gender of words. There are other rules for gender which you will learn as you study more Spanish.

1. Spanish words ending in *-o* are usually masculine.
2. Spanish words ending in *-a* are usually feminine.

Write the words on this page and the next page in the charts to determine their gender. Then, write the English words to the right. Use a Spanish-English dictionary if you need help.

Masculine	
words ending in *-o*	meaning of the word

maestra	maestro
amigo	amiga
silla	falda
rojo	abrigo
libro	vestido
ventana	camisa
puerta	chaqueta
cuaderno	sopa
escritorio	fruta
pluma	queso
anaranjado	tienda
blanco	museo
negro	casa

Nombre_____

Masculine and Feminine

Feminine	
words ending in *-a*	meaning of the word

maestra	maestro
amigo	amiga
silla	falda
rojo	abrigo
libro	vestido
ventana	camisa
puerta	chaqueta
cuaderno	sopa
escritorio	fruta
pluma	queso
anaranjado	tienda
blanco	museo
negro	casa

Nombre_____

More Than One

Spanish nouns can be placed into two groups—singular nouns (one of something) or plural nouns (more than one of something). Nouns that end in –s are usually plural. Nouns ending in other letters are usually singular.

Read the following familiar nouns. Write **S** if the noun is singular and **P** if the noun is plural.

_____ 1. calcetines   _____ 2. dedo   _____ 3. botas

_____ 4. cuerpo   _____ 5. vegetales   _____ 6. ciudad

_____ 7. escuela   _____ 8. sandalias   _____ 9. zapatos

_____ 10. guantes   _____ 11. casa   _____ 12. boca

Follow these rules to write the following Spanish words in the plural.

1. If the word ends in a vowel, add –s.
2. If the word ends in a consonant, add –es.
3. If the word ends in z, change the z to c before adding –es.

1. carne _____   6. nariz _____

2. silla _____   7. abrigo _____

3. ciudad _____   8. señor _____

4. lápiz _____   9. borrador _____

5. azul _____   10. pollo _____

Nombre_____

More and More

Write the plural form of each Spanish clue word in the puzzle.

Across

1. hombro
4. falda
5. zapato
7. museo
8. nariz
10. gato
11. sombrero
13. oso
14. lápiz

Down

2. borrador
3. vaso
6. escuela
9. casa
12. mesa

Nombre_____

Definite Articles

In Spanish, there are four ways to say "the"—*el, la, los,* and *las.* The definite article (the) agrees with its noun in gender (masculine or feminine) and number (singular or plural).

Masculine singular nouns go with *el.* Feminine singular nouns go with *la.*

Examples: *el libro* (the book)   *el papel* (the paper)
la silla (the chair)   *la regla* (the ruler)

Masculine plural nouns go with *los.* Feminine plural nouns go with *las.*

Examples: *los libros* (the books)   *los papeles* (the papers)
las sillas (the chairs)   *las reglas* (the rulers)

Refer to the Word Bank to complete the chart. Write the singular and plural forms and the correct definite articles. The first ones have been done for you.

Word Bank	cuaderno mesa pluma oso falda
	papel gato bota silla libro

English	Masculine Singular	Masculine Plural
the book	el libro	los libros
the paper		
the notebook		
the cat		
the bear		

English	Feminine Singular	Feminine Plural
the chair	la silla	las sillas
the table		
the boot		
the skirt		
the pen		

Nombre_____

Indefinite Articles

In English, the words *a*, *an*, and *some* are indefinite articles. In Spanish, there are four indefinite articles—*un, una, unas,* and *unos.*

Masculine singular nouns go with *un*. Feminine singular nouns go with *una.*

Examples: un *libro* (a book)   una *silla* (a chair)
un *papel* (a paper)   una *mesa* (a table)

Masculine plural nouns go with *unos*. Feminine plural nouns go with *unas.*

Examples: unos *libros* (some books)   unas *sillas* (some chairs)
unos *papeles* (some papers)   unas *mesas* (some tables)

Refer to the Word Bank to complete the chart. Write the singular and plural forms and the correct indefinite articles. The first one has been done for you.

Word Bank	cuaderno mesa pluma oso falda
	papel gato bota silla libro

English	Masculine Singular	Masculine Plural
a book	un libro	unos libros
a paper		
a notebook		
a cat		
a bear		

English	Feminine Singular	Feminine Plural
a chair		
a table		
a boot		
a skirt		
a pen		

Nombre_____

Articles and Nouns

Refer to the given articles and nouns to translate the following phrases into Spanish. Use a Spanish-English dictionary if you need help.

Articles			
un	una	unos	unas
el	la	los	las

Nouns			
cine (m)	cuerpo	museo	cuadernos
cara	falda	boca	caballos
blusa	elefantes (m)	tijeras	camas
dedo	cucharas		

1. a skirt _____

2. the body _____

3. the spoons _____

4. the mouth _____

5. the elephants _____

6. some scissors _____

7. the finger _____

8. a museum _____

9. the face _____

10. a blouse _____

11. the horses _____

12. some notebooks _____

13. the beds _____

14. a movie theater _____

Pretty Colors

Adjectives are words that tell about or describe nouns. Color each box as indicated in Spanish. Use a Spanish-English dictionary if you need help.

rojo	azul	verde	anaranjado	morado
amarillo	marrón	negro	blanco	rosado

Here are some new adjectives. Copy the Spanish adjectives in the boxes. Write the Spanish words next to the English words at the bottom of the page.

bonita	pretty	feo	ugly
grande	big	pequeño	small
limpio	clean	sucio	dirty
viejo	old	nuevo	new
feliz	happy	triste	sad

old _____   pretty _____   sad _____

big _____   small _____   happy _____

new _____   dirty _____   ugly _____

clean _____

Nombre_____

Abundant Adjectives

Circle the Spanish words you find in the word search. Then, write the English meanings next to the Spanish words at the bottom of the page.

v	v	é	o	i	x	q	g	r	r	d	s	a	h	o
e	i	f	o	l	b	p	q	u	s	e	n	a	v	y
r	r	e	a	r	r	l	m	b	k	n	a	q	e	r	a
d	j	c	s	o	g	i	h	o	r	n	u	y	b	d
e	o	r	b	i	s	e	r	a	n	n	f	h	i	o
y	x	o	x	b	n	a	n	a	a	i	c	h	c	q
f	t	l	v	v	x	j	d	l	m	l	t	x	b	j
e	o	o	o	p	a	o	c	o	i	a	ó	a	i	o
l	l	c	i	d	ñ	e	k	m	d	m	l	g	y	e
i	m	e	o	e	o	e	o	e	m	o	p	w	r	f
z	h	d	u	c	d	r	t	l	a	k	i	i	y	e
i	b	q	n	n	a	s	j	n	r	z	s	c	o	z
u	e	a	a	d	i	y	g	r	r	x	m	b	u	z
p	l	r	o	r	d	f	u	b	ó	o	j	o	r	s
b	g	s	t	v	u	k	v	y	n	s	l	u	z	a

rojo _____   marrón _____   azul _____

limpio _____   feo _____   sucio _____

pequeño _____   viejo _____   negro _____

amarillo _____   anaranjado _____   triste _____

grande _____   blanco _____   rosado _____

morado _____   nuevo _____   verde _____

feliz _____   bonita _____

Nombre_____

Words to Describe

Descriptive adjectives are words that describe nouns. On this page and the next page, write the Spanish adjective that describes each picture.

Word Bank

feliz	grande	nuevo	pequeño	feo	rica
limpio	sucio	bonita	triste	viejo	pobre
alto	bajo	abierto	cerrado		

large

_____

new

_____

ugly

_____

happy

_____

old

_____

sad

_____

small

_____

clean

_____

Nombre_____

Words to Describe

Word Bank

feliz	grande	nuevo	pequeño	feo	rica
limpio	sucio	bonita	triste	viejo	pobre
alto	bajo	abierto	cerrado		

pretty

dirty

tall

open

rich

short

closed

poor

Nombre_____

Words to Describe

Write the Spanish words for the clue words in the crossword puzzle.

Across

3. poor
7. open
9. tall
11. clean
12. dirty
13. new

Down

1. ugly
2. closed
4. happy
5. pretty
6. large
8. old
10. sad

Word Bank

viejo	grande
limpio	nuevo
bonita	triste
abierto	cerrado
alto	sucio
pobre	feliz
feo	

Nombre_____

Open and Close

Would you know what to do if your teacher told you to do something in Spanish? In each box, copy the Spanish word. Then, write the English word below it from the Word Bank.

Word Bank

sing	sit down	close	glue	open
stop	cut	paint	stand up	draw

corten

_____

_____

peguen

_____

_____

pinten

_____

_____

canten

_____

_____

abran

_____

_____

cierren

_____

_____

levántense

_____

_____

siéntense

_____

_____

paren

_____

_____

dibujen

_____

_____

Nombre_____

Write It Down

Write the Spanish word for each clue in the crossword puzzle.

Across

3. paint
4. open
7. stand up

8. sing
9. paste

Down

1. draw
2. sit down

5. close
6. stop

Word Bank

canten	cierren	levántense
paren	pinten	abran
siéntense	peguen	dibujen

Nombre_____

See It, Say It

On your turn roll the die, move your marker, and give the command in Spanish.

• If you can't remember a Spanish word, ask for help and skip a turn.

• The winner is the first player to reach the finish.

• This game is for two to four players.

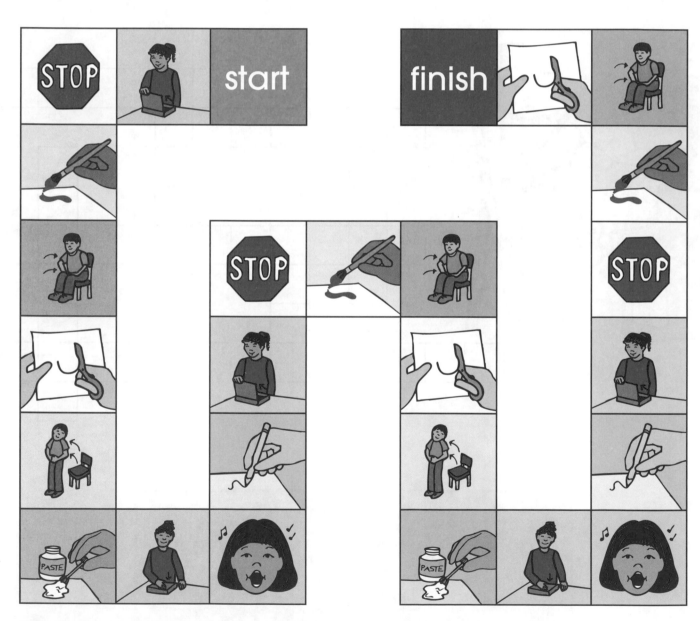

Nombre_____

Simon Says

Would you know what to do if your teacher asked you to do something in Spanish? On this page and the next page, copy the Spanish word. Then, write the English meaning below it.

Word Bank

sit down	glue	paint	close	run	listen
open	stand up	cut	walk	write	read

siéntense

_____

_____

abran

_____

_____

levántense

_____

_____

pinten

_____

_____

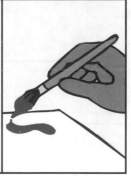

peguen

_____

_____

corten

_____

_____

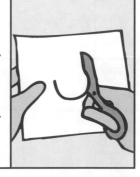

Nombre_____

Simon Says

Word Bank

sit down	glue	paint	close	run	listen
open	stand up	cut	walk	write	read

cierren

_____

_____

caminen

_____

_____

escriban

_____

_____

escuchen

_____

_____

corran

_____

_____

lean

_____

_____

Nombre_____

Search and Find

Circle the Spanish words you find in the word search. Write the English meanings at the bottom of the page next to the Spanish words from the puzzle.

n	l	p	p	u	m	d	o	c	n	a	n	n	p	v
j	g	a	j	n	a	v	o	e	s	e	e	j	i	o
b	t	v	g	r	c	r	l	i	n	j	e	l	n	l
e	f	b	o	f	r	i	é	i	u	b	o	x	t	t
p	s	k	a	a	a	n	m	b	a	j	m	d	e	e
e	c	n	n	b	t	a	i	n	r	o	h	r	n	e
g	n	b	e	e	c	d	c	c	x	u	p	n	x	n
u	r	c	n	t	b	n	t	a	o	i	j	a	n	s
e	m	s	e	h	n	r	n	e	n	r	g	e	r	e
n	e	i	y	x	j	á	i	e	s	t	t	l	o	i
y	t	g	o	l	c	q	v	n	r	n	e	e	p	m
r	n	r	n	h	c	m	e	e	q	r	e	n	n	b
a	b	r	a	n	t	u	p	k	l	u	e	r	e	r
o	y	p	n	e	h	c	u	c	s	e	e	i	a	w
x	u	n	u	n	a	b	i	r	c	s	e	n	c	p

Spanish Word	English	Spanish Word	English
corten	_____	corran	_____
levántense	_____	escriban	_____
peguen	_____	abran	_____
siéntense	_____	escuchen	_____
caminen	_____	cierren	_____
pinten	_____	lean	_____

Nombre_____

Action Words

In each box, copy the Spanish action verbs. Then, write the English word below it.

Word Bank

to touch	to look at	to eat	to give
to drink	to speak	to clean	to sleep

comer

_____

_____

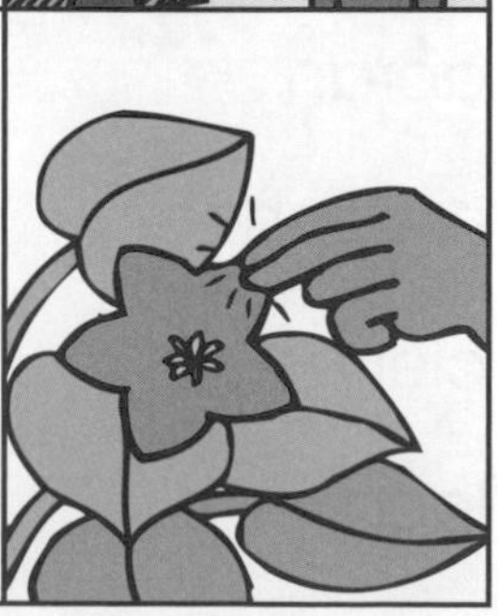

hablar

_____

_____

beber

_____

_____

limpiar

_____

_____

dormir

_____

_____

mirar

_____

_____

tocar

_____

_____

dar

_____

_____

Nombre_____

Action Words

Write the Spanish words from the Word Bank that fit in these word blocks. Write the English meanings below the blocks.

Word Bank

mirar	limpiar	tocar	beber
hablar	comer	dar	dormir

1.

_____

2.

_____

3.

_____

4.

_____

5.

_____

6.

_____

7.

_____

8.

_____

English

to eat	to look at	to speak	to touch
to clean	to sleep	to drink	to give

Nombre_____

First Sentences

Create original sentences in Spanish using the sentence starters and the verbs in the Word Bank. You may use one sentence starter more than once. Write the English meanings on the lines below the Spanish.

Word Bank

comer	beber	dormir	tocar
hablar	limpiar	mirar	dar

Sentence Starters

Me gusta _____ .   (I like _____ .)

No me gusta _____ .   (I don't like _____ .)

Quiero _____ .   (I want _____ .)

Necesito _____ .   (I need _____ .)

1. _____

   _____

2. _____

   _____

3. _____

   _____

4. _____

   _____

5. _____

   _____

Nombre_____

Action Words

On this page and the next page, refer to the Word Bank to write the Spanish word that matches each picture.

Word Bank

comer	beber	mirar	tocar
hablar	limpiar	trabajar	dar
estudiar	dormir	jugar	ir

to clean

to touch

to speak

to watch

to eat

_____

to drink

_____

Nombre_____

Action Words

Word Bank	comer	beber	mirar	tocar
	hablar	limpiar	trabajar	dar
	estudiar	dormir	jugar	ir

to give

_____

to sleep

_____

to go

_____

to work

_____

to study

_____

to play

_____

Nombre_____

Reading and Writing

Circle the Spanish words that you find in the word search. Write the English meanings at the bottom of the page next to the Spanish words from the puzzle.

r	c	c	i	r	h	x	n	l	e	p	r
t	e	o	o	e	d	z	u	s	r	e	l
r	b	m	i	n	h	x	t	a	b	r	i
a	s	s	o	g	t	u	d	e	w	c	m
b	v	g	c	c	d	e	b	w	r	i	p
a	s	v	y	i	r	r	s	j	e	b	i
j	r	v	a	a	h	q	i	t	e	r	a
a	e	r	c	a	r	r	u	m	a	e	r
r	v	s	b	a	b	u	a	i	r	r	r
s	u	l	g	i	b	i	z	r	t	o	o
b	a	u	g	g	w	n	a	j	i	a	d
r	j	n	d	x	r	a	c	o	t	m	r

Spanish Word	English	Spanish Word	English
comer	_____	jugar	_____
hablar	_____	dormir	_____
estudiar	_____	mirar	_____
beber	_____	trabajar	_____
limpiar	_____	tocar	_____
ir	_____	dar	_____

Capital Letters

Spanish uses capital letters less often than English. Follow these rules as your guide.

> ### Capitalization Rules
>
> 1. All Spanish sentences begin with capital letters.
> 2. Names of people begin with capital letters.
> 3. Names of places (cities, regions, countries, continents) and holidays begin with capital letters.
> 4. Titles are not capitalized unless abbreviated (*señor–Sr., usted–Ud.*).
> 5. Some words that are normally capitalized in English may not be capitalized in Spanish (nationalities, religions, languages, months, and days).

Write *sí* if the word should be capitalized. Write *no* if it should remain lowercase.

1. sarah _____
2. inglés _____
3. navidad _____
4. español _____
5. mexicano _____
6. africa _____
7. señor _____
8. enero _____

9. domingo _____
10. católico _____
11. santa fé _____
12. viernes _____
13. méxico _____
14. julio _____
15. colorado _____
16. miguel _____

Nombre_____

Categories

Read the list of words given. Write the words in the proper columns. If the word needs a capital letter, write it that way.

los angeles	susana	santa fé	señora
maría	sr.	océano pacífico	josé
uds.	sra.	juan	mexicano
inglés	viernes	septiembre	lunes
san diego	cuba	americano	méxico
señorita	ustedes	américa del norte	católico
españa	san antonio	español	señor

People	Places	Titles	Not Capitalized

Nombre_____

Introductions and Greetings

¡Hola!

¿Cómo te llamas?

Me llamo...

Introductions and Greetings

¿Cómo estás?

bien

así, así

¡Adiós!

mal

Introductions and Greetings

Say the Spanish introductions and greetings out loud.

¡Hola! Hello

¿Cómo te llamas?  What is your name?

Me llamo...  My name is...

¿Cómo estás?..  How are you?

 bien

 mal

 así, así

¡Adiós! Good-bye

Nombre_____

Pictures of Greetings

Say the greeting out loud. Circle the picture that tells the meaning of each word.

¡Hola!		
¿Cómo te llamas?		
Me llamo...		
¿Cómo estás?..		
bien		
mal		
así, así		
¡Adiós!		

Greetings Paste Up

Cut out a picture from a magazine that shows the meaning of each greeting and glue it next to the correct word or words.

¡Hola!

¿Cómo te llamas?

Me llamo...

¿Cómo estás?..

bien

mal

así, así

¡Adiós!

Nombre_____

Polite Words

Say each Spanish expression out loud.

¿Cuántos años tienes?		How old are you?
Tengo seis años.		I am six years old.
por favor		please
gracias		thank you

amigo  friend amiga friend

sí no amigos  friends

¡Hasta luego!  See you later!

Nombre_____

Introductions and Greetings Review

Say each expression out loud. Circle the picture that tells the meaning of each word.

gracias			
Tengo seis años.			
por favor			
amigo			
amigos			
¡Hasta luego!			
amiga			
sí			

Nombre_____

What's Your Name?

Word Bank		
I'm so–so.	What's your name?	I'm well/fine.
I'm ____ years old.	I'm not doing well.	My name is ___.
I'm not well.	How are you?	How old are you?

Refer to the Word Bank to translate the Spanish questions and answers into English.

1. ¿Cómo te llamas? _____

    Me llamo _____

2. ¿Cómo estás? _____

    Estoy bien/mal/así así. _____

3. ¿Cuántos años tienes? _____

    Tengo ___ años. _____

Word Bank			
hello	please	friend	yes
no	thank you	goodbye	See you later!

Write the English meaning after the Spanish word.

4. hola _____   8. por favor _____

5. amigo, amiga _____   9. gracias _____

6. sí _____   10. ¡Hasta luego! _____

7. no _____   11. adiós _____

Nombre_____

Word Blocks

Write the Spanish words from the Word Bank that fit in the word blocks.
Don't forget the punctuation. Write the English meanings below the blocks.

1.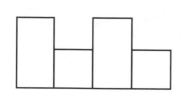

_____

2.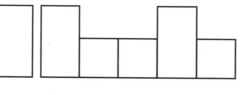

_____

3.

_____

4.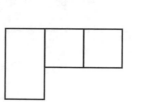

5.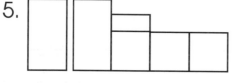

_____

6.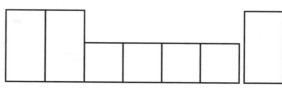

_____

7.

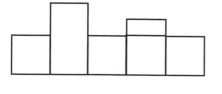

8.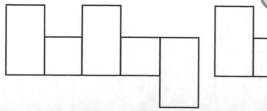

Spanish Word Bank

por favor	adiós	Estoy bien.
hola	¡Hasta luego!	¿Cómo te llamas?
no	¿Cómo estás?	

Nombre_____

Greetings

Use the Word Bank to write the English meaning of the Spanish words and phrases.

1. señor _____

2. señora _____

3. señorita _____

4. maestro _____

5. maestra _____

6. ¡Buenos días! _____

7. ¡Buenas tardes! _____

8. ¡Buenas noches! _____

9. Vamos a contar. _____

Word Bank

Mr.	Good night!	Good morning!
Good afternoon!	teacher (female)	teacher (male)
Miss	Let's count.	Mrs.

Draw a picture to show the time of day that you use each expression.

¡Buenos días!	¡Buenas tardes!	¡Buenas noches!

Nombre_____

Spanish Greetings

Write the Spanish word for each clue in the crossword puzzle.

Across
1. bad
4. good
7. teacher (male)
9. friend (female)
10. Mr.
11. Miss

Down
2. friend (male)
3. hello
5. thank you
6. goodbye
7. teacher (female)
8. Mrs.

Word Bank

amiga	mal
señora	señor
maestra	bien
adiós	hola
señorita	gracias
amigo	maestro

Nombre_____

Greetings

Refer to the Word Bank to translate the Spanish greetings, questions, and answers.

¡Buenos días! _____

¡Buenas tardes! _____

¡Buenas noches! _____

¿Cómo estás? _____

    bien, gracias _____

    mal _____

    así así _____

¿Cómo te llamas? _____

    Me llamo _____ . _____

¿Cuántos años tienes? _____

    Tengo _____ años. _____

adiós _____ hola _____

Word Bank

goodbye
Good morning!
I am ____ years old.
fine, thank you
Good afternoon!
hello
How old are you?
How are you?
What is your name?
My name is ____ .
not well
ok/so-so
Good night!

Word Bank

teacher (m/f)	Miss	no
Mr.	friend (m/f)	please
Mrs.	yes	

Refer to the Word Bank to translate the Spanish vocabulary.

amigo/amiga _____

sí _____ no _____ por favor _____

señor _____ señora _____

maestro/maestra _____

señorita _____

Nombre_____

Find the Words

Circle the Spanish words that you find in the word search. Then, write the English meanings at the bottom of the page next to the Spanish words from the puzzle.

y	q	d	t	h	s	a	s	s	n	m	m
o	w	m	o	r	m	e	e	x	o	a	a
m	o	l	o	i	ñ	ñ	h	k	n	e	e
u	a	ñ	g	o	o	m	p	k	k	s	s
q	e	a	r	r	u	g	l	o	l	t	t
s	s	i	a	b	m	w	h	z	e	r	r
s	t	a	a	a	m	n	v	e	m	o	a
a	w	i	i	d	m	x	i	í	j	d	j
x	b	o	l	c	i	i	n	s	i	x	x
w	t	q	f	v	a	ó	g	e	l	t	u
t	o	n	m	s	h	r	s	o	i	a	k
m	g	b	f	n	f	z	g	w	u	b	m

Spanish Word	English	Spanish Word	English
amigo	_____	adiós	_____
gracias	_____	maestro	_____
mal	_____	señor	_____
amiga	_____	bien	_____
hola	_____	maestra	_____
no	_____	señora	_____
señorita	_____	sí	_____

Days

lunes   miércoles   viernes   domingo

martes   jueves   sábado

Monday	Tuesday	Wednesday	Thursday	Friday	Saturday	Sunday
		1	2	3	4	5
6	7	8	9	10	11	12
13	14	15	16	17	18	19
20	21	22	23	24	25	26
27	28	29	30			

Months

enero

febrero

marzo

abril

mayo

junio

julio

agosto

septiembre

octubre

noviembre

diciembre

Nombre_____

Seven Days

Copy the Spanish words for the days of the week. In Spanish-speaking countries, lunes is the first day of the week.

Monday	**lunes**	_____
Tuesday	**martes**	_____
Wednesday	**miércoles**	_____
Thursday	**jueves**	_____
Friday	**viernes**	_____
Saturday	**sábado**	_____
Sunday	**domingo**	_____

Draw a line to match the Spanish and English days of the week.

Puzzle of the Week

Write the Spanish words in the puzzle.

Across
2. Thursday
7. Wednesday

Down
1. Monday
3. Saturday
4. Friday
5. Sunday
6. Tuesday

Word Bank

jueves	domingo	martes
sábado	viernes	lunes
	miércoles	

Nombre_____

Calendar Game

On your turn roll the die, move your marker, and say the number and day of the week in Spanish.

• If you can't remember a Spanish word, ask for help and skip a turn.

• To win, be the first to translate a date from the bottom row.

• This game is for two to four players.

Monday	Tuesday	Wednesday	Thursday	Friday	Saturday	Sunday
	start	1	2	3	4	5
6	7	8	9	10	11	12
13	14	15	16	17	18	19
20	21	22	23	24	25	26
27	28	29	30			

finish line

Rain in April

Refer to the Word Bank to write the Spanish word for the given month. Then, in the box, draw a picture of something that happens in that month of the year. Remember that Spanish months do not begin with capital letters.

Word Bank

agosto	septiembre	noviembre	mayo
junio	enero	octubre	febrero
marzo	julio	diciembre	abril

January		July	
_____		_____	
February		August	
_____		_____	
March		September	
_____		_____	
April		October	
_____		_____	
May		November	
_____		_____	
June		December	
_____		_____	

Nombre_____

Writing Practice

Copy the following paragraph. Then, practice reading it out loud.

Hay doce meses en un año. Diciembre, enero, y febrero son en el invierno. Marzo, abril, y mayo son en la primavera. Junio, julio, y agosto son en el verano. Septiembre, octubre, y noviembre son en el otoño. ¿Cual es tu mes favorito del año?

Nombre_____

Spanish Months

Write the Spanish word for the clue words in the crossword puzzle. Use the Word Bank at the bottom of the page.

Across

4. July
9. May
10. September
11. June
12. January

Down

1. April
2. November
3. December
5. March
6. February
7. August
8. October

Word Bank

marzo	mayo	diciembre	junio
septiembre	octubre	julio	agosto
abril	enero	febrero	noviembre

Colors

negro

blanco

azul

verde

amarillo

Colors

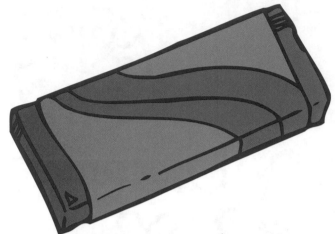

marrón

anaranjado

rojo

morado

rosado

Nombre_____

Colors

Say the words out loud. Color each word with the correct color.

Nombre_____

Pictures to Color

Color the pictures according to each color word.

rojo

azul

verde

anaranjado

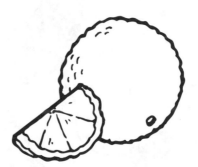

morado

amarillo

Nombre_____

Rainbow Colors

Color the picture according to the color words shown.

Nombre_____

Color the Cars

Color the cars according to the color words shown.

rojo

azul

verde

morado

anaranjado

amarillo

Nombre_____

Birds of Color

Color the birds according to the words shown.

Nombre_____

House of Colors

Color each crayon with the correct color for the Spanish word. Draw something with your favorite color.

☐ rojo   ☐ negro   ☐ marrón   ☐ rosado
☐ azul   ☐ amarillo   ☐ blanco   ☐ verde

Nombre_____

Color the Flowers

Color each flower with the correct color for the Spanish word.

☐ azul ☐ marrón ☐ amarillo ☐ rosado
☐ verde ☐ rojo ☐ morado ☐ anaranjado

Color Search

Cut out pictures from a magazine that match the colors below. Glue each picture next to the correct color word.

rojo		amarillo	
azul		marrón	
verde		negro	
anaranjado		blanco	
morado		rosado	

Nombre_____

Moving Colors

Color the pictures according to the words shown.

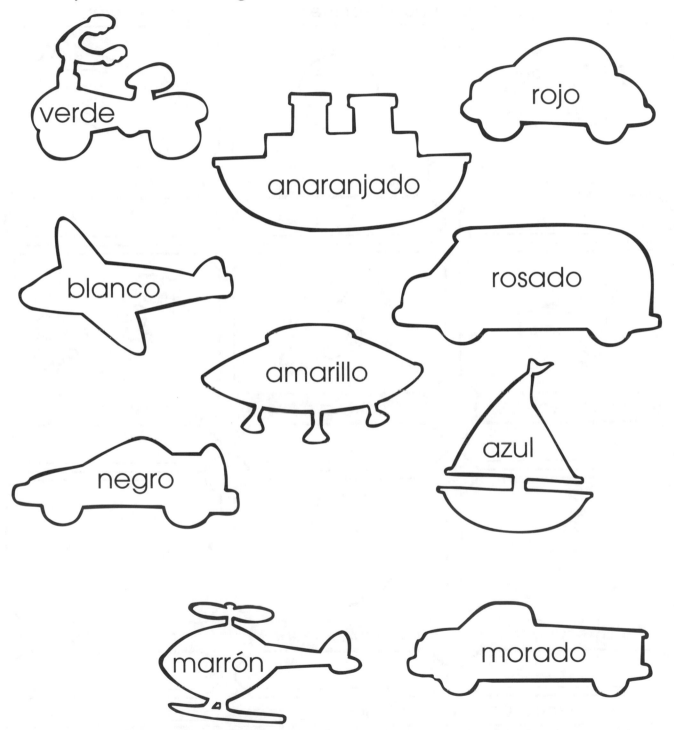

verde

anaranjado

rojo

blanco

rosado

amarillo

negro

azul

marrón

morado

What is your favorite color? (Answer in Spanish.) _____

Nombre_____

Color Away

Write the English word below the Spanish color listed. Use the words at the bottom of the page to help you. Color the pictures using that color.

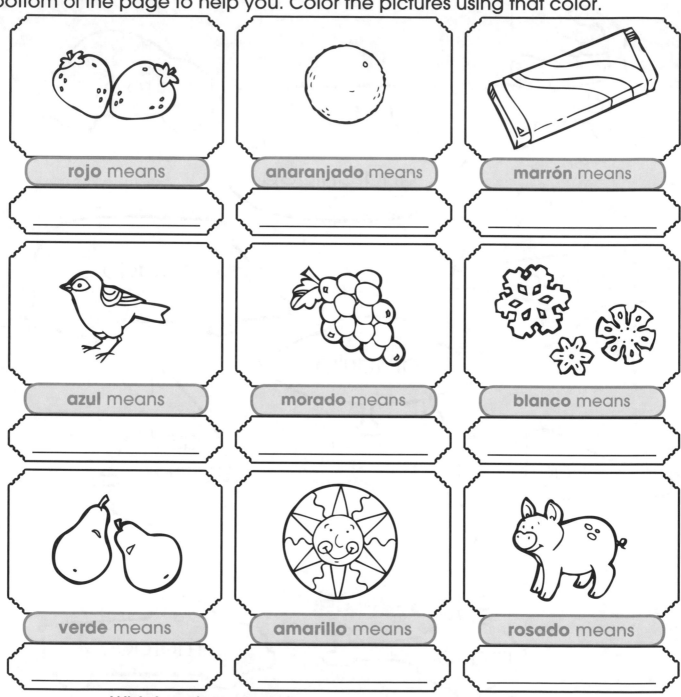

| rojo means | anaranjado means | marrón means |
| _____ | _____ | _____ |

| azul means | morado means | blanco means |
| _____ | _____ | _____ |

| verde means | amarillo means | rosado means |
| _____ | _____ | _____ |

Which color was not used? _____

white	red	orange	green	pink
blue	purple	yellow	brown	black

Nombre_____

Color Crossword

Write the correct Spanish color words in the spaces.
Use the Word Bank at the bottom of the page.
Follow the English color clues.

ACROSS

3. yellow
5. purple
6. black
8. white
9. pink

DOWN

1. blue
2. red
4. orange
7. green

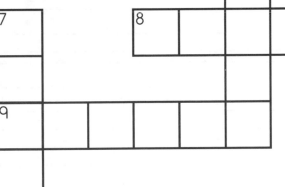

blanco	rojo	anaranjado	verde	rosado
azul	morado	amarillo	negro	

Nombre_____

Color Copy

Copy the following words in the color of each word.
Which word is hard to see with the actual color? _____

rojo

azul

verde

anaranjado

morado

amarillo

marrón

negro

blanco

rosado

Nombre_____

Colorful Flowers

Color the flowers according to the Spanish color words shown below.

Nombre_____

Color Find

Circle the Spanish color words that you find in the word search. Then, write the English meaning of each word.

é	o	a	p	v	o	r	n	u	a	j	v
m	c	x	z	q	d	b	i	a	r	e	a
a	n	n	a	u	i	g	y	i	r	n	n
r	a	c	a	m	l	c	j	d	a	j	y
r	l	o	t	l	a	i	e	r	z	o	r
ó	b	g	r	d	b	r	a	t	f	g	l
n	q	d	b	v	o	n	i	s	b	b	f
o	v	s	d	d	j	h	n	l	u	f	o
c	m	y	a	a	o	k	x	e	l	t	j
e	t	r	d	i	o	c	n	k	g	o	o
d	o	o	p	w	q	s	i	d	x	r	r
m	r	o	s	a	d	o	q	k	k	t	o

Spanish Word	English	Spanish Word	English
blanco	_____	amarillo	_____
azul	_____	verde	_____
rojo	_____	marrón	_____
morado	_____	rosado	_____
anaranjado	_____	negro	_____

Nombre_____

Draw and Color

In each box, write the Spanish color word. Use the Word Bank below to help you. Then, draw and color a picture of something that is that color.

red is _____	orange is _____	brown is _____
blue is _____	purple is _____	black is _____
green is _____	yellow is _____	pink is _____

Which Spanish color from the Word Bank is not used above? _____

Word Bank

blanco	rojo	amarillo	rosado
azul	morado	verde	negro
	anaranjado	marrón	

Nombre_____

Butterfly Garden

Color the butterfly garden as indicated in Spanish.

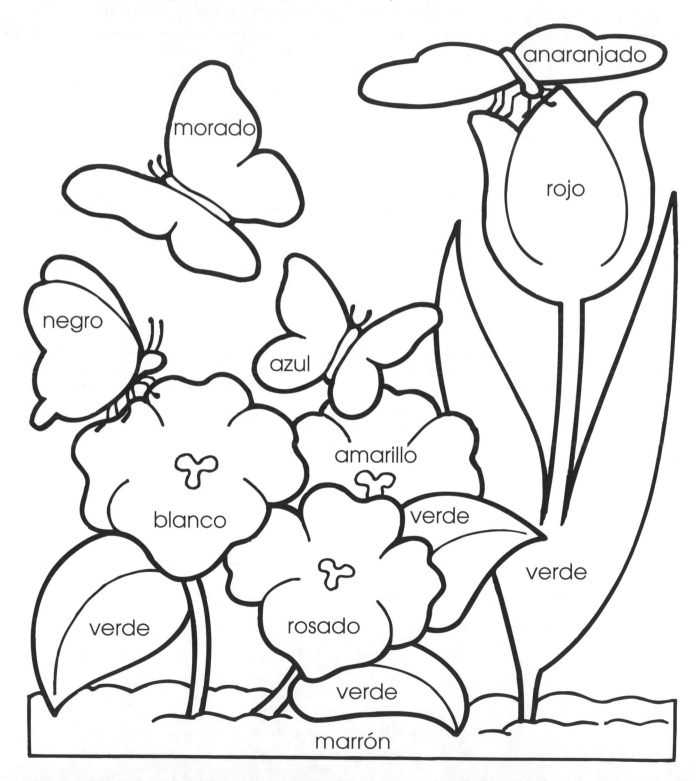

Nombre_____

Across the Spectrum

Write the Spanish for each clue word in the crossword puzzle.

Across

3. black
6. blue
7. red
8. purple
9. white
10. brown

Down

1. green
2. pink
4. yellow
5. orange

Food

leche

pollo

ensalada

Nombre_____

Food

queso

papa

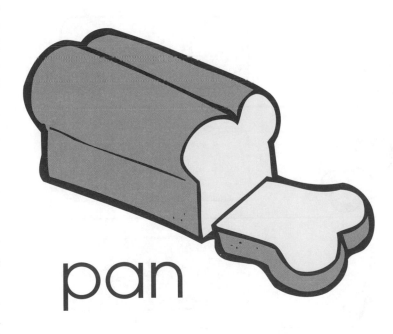

pan

jugo

Food and Drink

Say the Spanish words for some delicious foods and drinks out loud.

queso		cheese
leche		milk
papa		potato
jugo		juice
pan	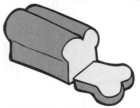	bread
pollo		chicken
ensalada		salad

My Meal

Draw or cut out pictures of food and glue them on the plate to make a meal. Which food is your favorite?

Mi comida

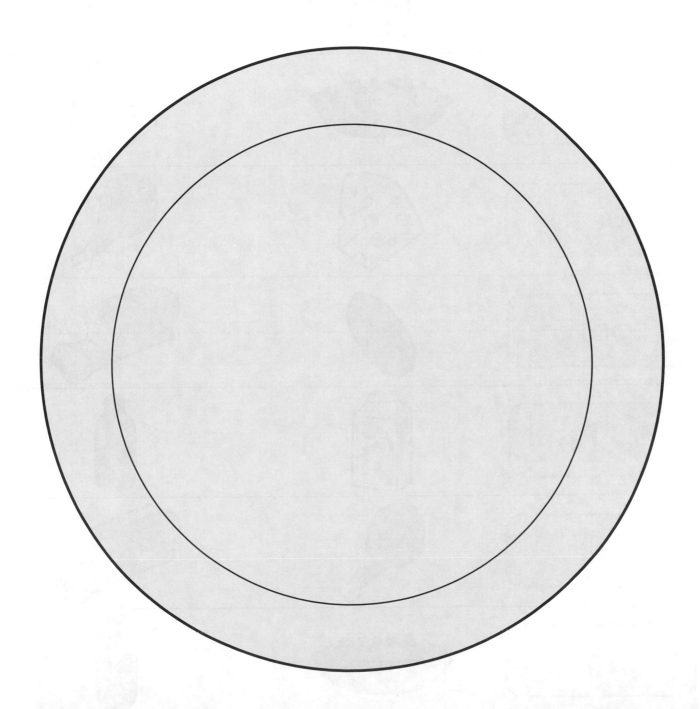

Food Meanings

Say each word out loud. Circle the picture that shows the meaning of each word.

papa		
ensalada		
queso		
pan		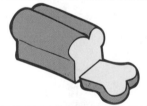
leche		
pollo		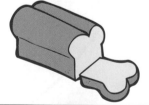
jugo		

Nombre_____

Mixed-Up Food

Draw a line from the word to the food picture.

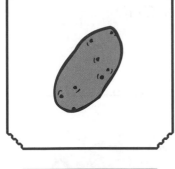

papa

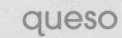
ensalada

queso

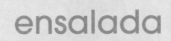
pan

leche

jugo

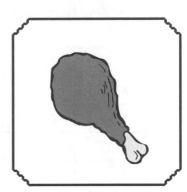

pollo

Food Words

Say each word out loud. Write the English word next to it.

queso _____

leche _____

papa _____

jugo

pan _____

pollo _____

ensalada _____

Color the blocks that have x's.
Do not color the blocks with numbers. What word did you find? _____

7	x	7	7	7	7	7	7	7	7	7	x	7	7	7	7	7	7	7
7	x	7	7	7	7	7	7	7	7	7	x	7	7	7	7	7	7	7
7	x	7	7	7	7	7	7	7	7	7	x	7	7	7	7	7	7	7
7	x	7	x	x	x	7	x	x	x	7	x	7	7	7	x	x	x	7
7	x	7	x	7	x	7	x	7	7	7	x	x	x	7	x	7	x	7
7	x	7	x	x	x	7	x	7	7	7	x	7	x	7	x	x	x	7
7	x	7	x	7	7	7	x	7	7	7	x	7	x	7	x	7	7	7
7	x	7	x	x	x	7	x	x	x	7	x	7	x	7	x	x	x	7

Food Riddles

Answer the riddles. Use the size and shape of the word blocks along with the answers at the bottom to help you.

I come from an animal. Kids like to eat my drumstick. What am I?

I can be full of holes. Mice like me. What am I?

I am squeezed from fruit. Apple is a popular flavor. What am I?

I come from a cow. I can be regular or chocolate. What am I?

You can eat me baked, fried, or mashed. What am I?

You can eat me plain or with dressing. What am I?

I rise while baking in an oven. What am I?

queso   leche
papa   ensalada   pan
pollo   jugo

Nombre_____

New Food Words

Say each word out loud. Copy each word and color the picture.

> sopa

> agua

> naranja

> carne

> plátano

> manzana

> sándwich

Use the Clues

Use the clues and the Word Bank at the bottom of the page to find the answers. Do not use any answer more than once.

1. You would not eat either of these fruits until you peel them.

_____   _____

2. Both of these drinks have a flavor.

_____   _____

3. You could put either of these on a sandwich.

_____   _____

4. These can be baked before eating. They all begin with the letter "p."

_____   _____   _____

5. These two go together on a cold winter day.

_____   _____

6. You use this liquid to wash this fruit.

_____   _____

7. Which word didn't you use?

_____

| queso | leche | papa | jugo | pan | pollo | ensalada |
| naranja | sopa | agua | sándwich | manzana | carne | plátano |

Check off each word as you use it.

Food   Nombre_____

A Square Meal

Refer to the Word Bank to write the name of each food in Spanish.

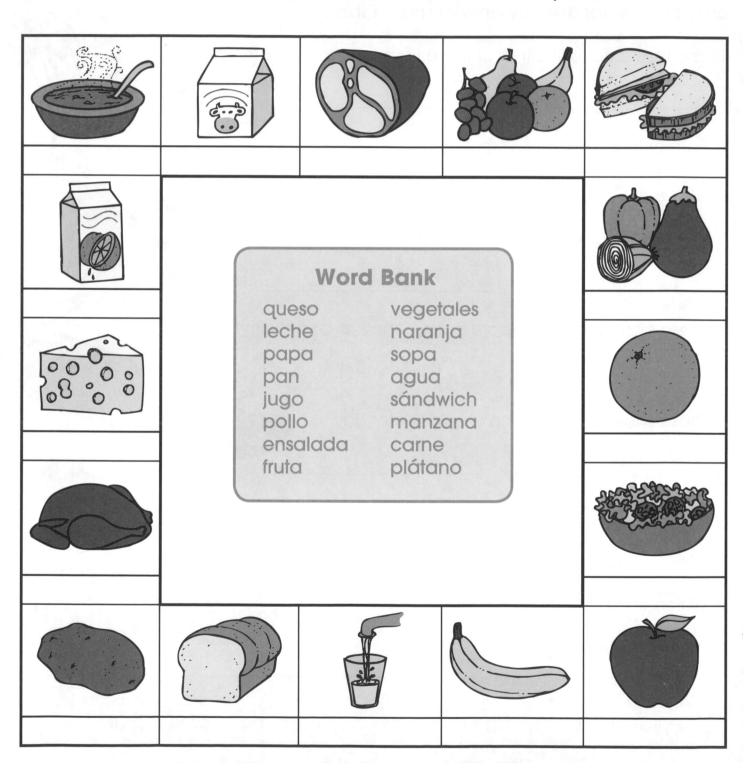

Word Bank

queso   vegetales
leche   naranja
papa   sopa
pan   agua
jugo   sándwich
pollo   manzana
ensalada   carne
fruta   plátano

Nombre_____

Searching for Food

Circle the Spanish words that you find in the word search. Then, write the English meaning of each word.

i	v	a	d	a	l	a	s	n	e	p	a
m	a	n	z	a	n	a	s	s	a	g	p
c	a	j	n	a	r	a	n	p	u	o	e
e	o	f	j	v	h	e	a	a	l	a	s
c	h	s	y	i	x	b	b	l	t	e	p
l	a	c	e	w	y	b	o	u	l	t	l
p	e	r	i	u	m	q	r	a	a	v	á
a	t	c	n	w	q	f	t	m	d	a	t
n	u	i	h	e	d	e	o	s	x	p	a
r	m	r	t	e	g	n	i	g	l	o	n
f	r	s	k	e	j	o	á	w	u	s	o
i	r	a	v	p	a	h	h	s	i	j	v

Spanish Word	English	Spanish Word	English
queso	_____	papa	_____
jugo	_____	ensalada	_____
sopa	_____	sándwich	_____
carne	_____	fruta	_____
leche	_____	pan	_____
pollo	_____	naranja	_____
agua	_____	manzana	_____
plátano	_____	vegetales	_____

Food Groups

On this page and the next page, write the Spanish food words to match the pictures.

Word Bank

ensalada	pan	sopa	sándwich
plátano	naranja	fruta	leche
manzana	queso	jugo	agua
papa	carne	vegetales	pollo

cheese	meat	soup

juice	vegetables	water

orange	bread

Nombre_____

Food Groups

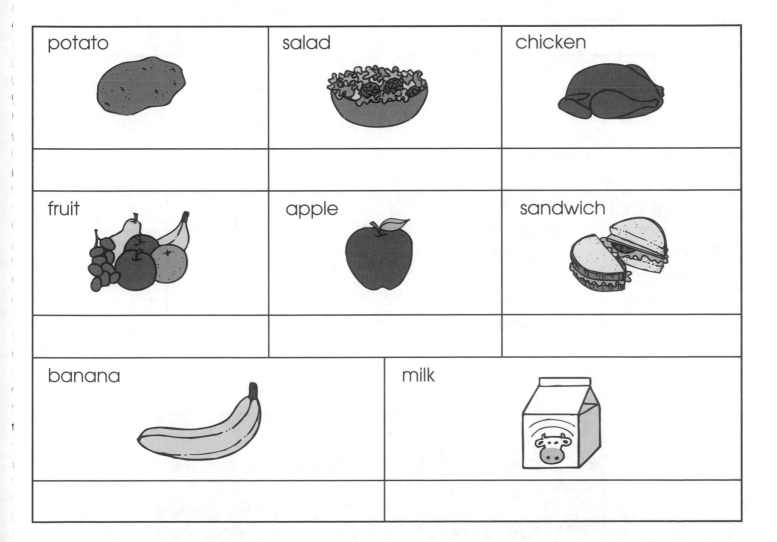

potato	salad	chicken
fruit	apple	sandwich
banana	milk	

Nombre_____

Eat It Up

Write the Spanish for the clue words in the crossword puzzle.

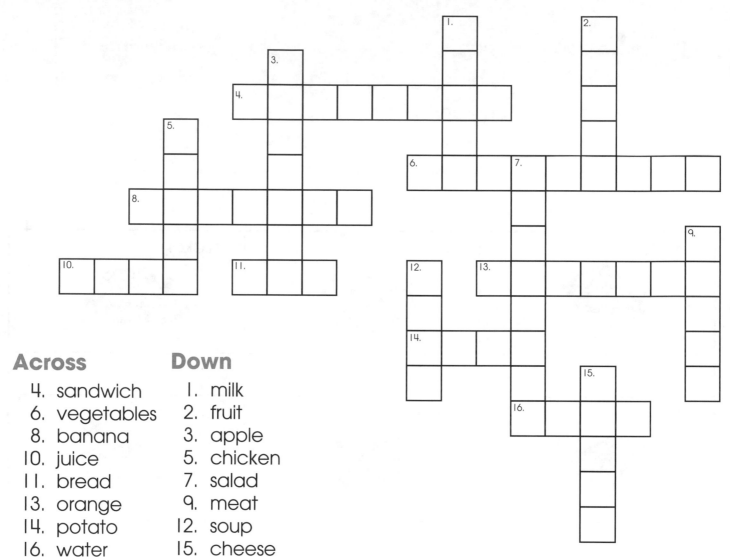

Across

4. sandwich
6. vegetables
8. banana
10. juice
11. bread
13. orange
14. potato
16. water

Down

1. milk
2. fruit
3. apple
5. chicken
7. salad
9. meat
12. soup
15. cheese

Word Bank

ensalada	plátano	manzana	papa
pan	naranja	fruta	queso
carne	sopa	jugo	vegetales
sándwich	leche	agua	pollo

Nombre_____

Animals

perro

pájaro

rana

pez

vaca

Animals

abeja

pato

gato

oso

caballo

Nombre_____

Animals All Around

Copy each word and color the pictures.

_____
- - - - - - - - - - - - - - - - - - -
_____

_____   > **perro**   _____
- - - - - - - - - - - - - - -   - - - - - - - - - - - - - - -
_____   _____

> **gato**   > **pájaro**

> **pez**   > **culebra**
   - - - - - - - - - - - - - - -
- - - - - - - - - - - - - - -   _____
_____

                              > **pato**

                              - - - - - - - - - - - - - - -
                              _____

Nombre_____

Animal Art

Choose four animals and draw each animal in its home. Label it with the Spanish animal word.

Nombre_____

Animal Crossword

Use the picture clues to complete the puzzle. Choose from the Spanish words at the bottom of the page. One is done for you.

| oso | perro | pájaro |
| pez | pato | culebra |

Nombre_____

Use the Clues

Answer the questions. Use the clues and the Spanish words at the bottom of the page. You may use answers more than once.

1. Both words begin with the same letter, and both animals have feathers.

_____   _____

2. These two animals walk and are house pets.

_____   _____

3. Both animals begin with the same letter. One quacks and the other barks.

_____   _____

4. Both of these animals like to live in the water.

_____   _____

5. These animals do not have fur or feathers.

_____   _____

6. The first animal likes to chase and catch the second animal. They both end with the letter *o*.

_____   _____

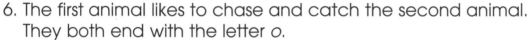

| gato | perro | pájaro |
| pez | pato | culebra |

Nombre_____

Animal Parade

In each box, copy the name of each animal in Spanish. Write the Spanish words next to the English words at the bottom of the page.

pájaro	bird
perro	dog
rana	frog
vaca	cow
abeja	bee

Write the Spanish words from above next to the English words.

dog _____   frog _____

bird _____   bee _____

cow _____

Nombre_____

Animal Parade

In each box, copy the name of each animal in Spanish. Write the Spanish words next to the English words at the bottom of the page.

caballo	horse
oso	bear
gato	cat
pato	duck
pez	fish

Write the Spanish words from above next to the English words.

cat _____   bear _____

fish _____   duck _____

horse _____

Nombre_____

Draw the Animals

Draw a picture to match the Spanish phrase in each box.

seis pájaros	cinco patos
nueve abejas	
tres gatos	diez ranas

Nombre_____

Draw the Animals

Draw a picture to match the Spanish phrase in each box.

cuatro perros	ocho caballos
siete osos	
dos vacas	un pez

Nombre_____

Name That Animal

On your turn roll the die, move your marker, and say the animal name in Spanish.

- If you can't remember a Spanish word, ask for help and skip a turn.
- The winner is the player to reach the finish first.
- For two to four players.

Nombre_____

Animal Match

Copy the Spanish word under each picture.

oso	rana	caballo	vaca

_____

elefante	oveja	puerco	gallina

_____

gato	tortuga	mariposa	dinosaurio

_____

Write the Spanish for each animal name.

1. butterfly _____
2. sheep _____
3. cat _____
4. dinosaur _____
5. chicken _____
6. pig _____
7. cow _____
8. bear _____
9. elephant _____
10. horse _____
11. turtle _____
12. frog _____

Nombre_____

Rainbow Roundup

Copy the following Spanish sentences on the lines provided. Then, write the English meanings.

1. El oso es blanco. _____

_____

2. El puerco es rosado. _____

_____

3. La rana es roja. _____

_____

4. La tortuga es verde. _____

_____

5. El dinosaurio es azul. _____

_____

6. El gato es anaranjado. _____

_____

7. La gallina es amarilla. _____

_____

8. El caballo es marrón. _____

_____

9. La mariposa es morada. _____

_____

Clothing

vestido

gorra

camisa

Clothing

calcetines

zapatos

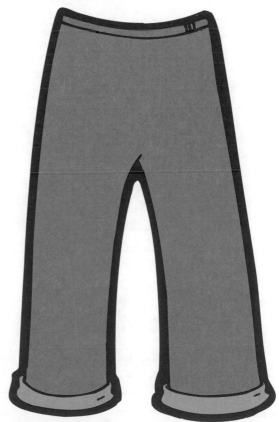

pantalones

Nombre_____

Clothing

Say each word out loud.

camisa		shirt
pantalones		pants
vestido		dress
calcetines		socks
zapatos		shoes
gorra		cap

Nombre_____

Clothing Match-Ups

Draw a line from the word to match the correct picture. Color the picture.

camisa

pantalones

zapatos

gorra

vestido

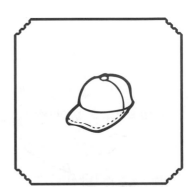

calcetines

Nombre_____

Who Are You?

Draw or cut out pictures of clothes to make a boy or girl. Write the names of the clothes next to them in Spanish.

Nombre_____

Cut Out Clothes

Cut out pictures and glue them next to the correct words.

camisa

zapatos

calcetines

vestido

pantalones

gorra

Color each block with a letter X inside. Do not color the blocks with numbers. What hidden word did you find? _____

8	8	8	8	8	8	8	8	8	8	8	8	8	8	8	8	8	8	8	8	8	8	8
8	8	x	x	x	8	x	x	x	8	x	x	x	8	x	x	x	8	x	x	x	8
8	8	x	8	x	8	x	8	x	8	x	8	x	8	x	8	x	8	x	8	x	8
8	8	x	x	x	8	x	8	x	8	x	8	8	8	x	8	8	8	x	8	x	8
8	8	8	8	x	8	x	x	x	8	x	8	8	8	x	8	8	8	x	x	x	x
8	8	x	8	x	8	8	8	8	8	8	8	8	8	8	8	8	8	8	8	8	8
8	8	x	x	x	8	8	8	8	8	8	8	8	8	8	8	8	8	8	8	8	8

Nombre_____

Clothing

Say each word out loud. Copy each word and color the picture.

pantalones

gorra

vestido

camisa

zapatos

calcetines

Nombre_____

Clothing

Say each word out loud. Copy each word and color the picture.

_____
- - - - - - - - - - - - - - - -
_____

_____
- - - - - - - - - - - - - - - -
_____

▶ abrigo

_____
- - - - - - - - - - - - - - - -
_____

▶ chaqueta

▶ falda

▶ guantes

▶ pantalones cortos

▶ botas

_____
- - - - - - - - - - - - - - - -
_____

_____
- - - - - - - - - - - - - - - -
_____

_____
- - - - - - - - - - - - - - - -
_____

Nombre_____

Remember These?

Fill in the blanks with the missing letters. Use the Spanish clothing words at the bottom to help you.

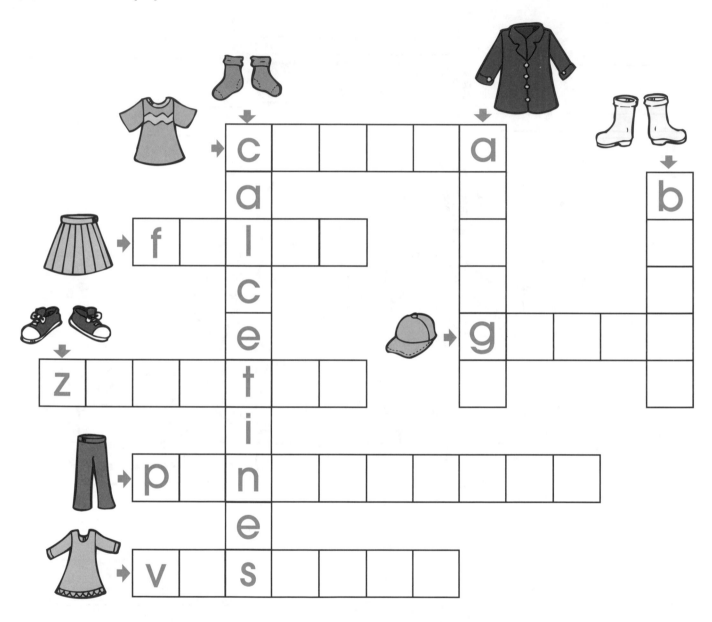

calcetines camisa   vestido   pantalones
falda   zapatos   gorra   abrigo
botas

Nombre_____

What Belongs?

Circle the item that does not belong with the other two. Write the name in Spanish below its picture.

_____

_____

What Belongs?

Circle the two items that are alike. Say the item in Spanish that is not like the other two. Color the pictures.

Nombre_____

Clothes Closet

On this page and the next page, refer to the Word Bank and write the Spanish word for each item of clothing pictured.

Word Bank

vestido	cinturón	pantalones
sombrero	pantalones cortos	zapatos
guantes	botas	chaqueta
calcetines	falda	camisa

shirt	shorts

socks	shoes

boots	gloves

Nombre_____

Clothes Closet

Word Bank

vestido	cinturón	pantalones
sombrero	pantalones cortos	zapatos
guantes	botas	chaqueta
calcetines	falda	camisa

pants 	hat 

skirt 	belt 

dress 	jacket 

Nombre_____

Dressing Up

Write the Spanish word for each clue in the crossword puzzle.

Across
1. shoes
4. socks
7. dress
8. gloves
9. hat
10. shirt

Word Bank

cinturón	botas	camisa
guantes	calcetines	sombrero
chaqueta	falda	zapatos
pantalones	vestido	

Down
2. pants
3. skirt
4. jacket
5. belt
6. boots

Nombre_____

Colorful Clothing

Copy each sentence in Spanish on the first line. Write the English meaning on the second line.

1. El vestido es rojo. _____

    _____

2. La camisa es marrón. _____

    _____

3. El sombrero es morado. _____

    _____

4. La falda es verde. _____

    _____

5. El vestido es rosado. _____

    _____

6. La chaqueta es azul. _____

    _____

7. Los calcetines son amarillos. _____

    _____

8. El cinturón es anaranjado. _____

    _____

9. Las botas son blancas. _____

    _____

Nombre_____

Matching Clothes

Underneath each picture, write the English word that matches the Spanish and the pictures. Write the Spanish words next to the English words at the bottom of the page.

falda	zapatos
abrigo	calcetines
guantes	pantalones
gorra	sandalias

1. skirt _____

2. socks _____

3. coat _____

4. sandals _____

5. cap _____

6. pants _____

7. gloves _____

8. shoes _____

Nombre_____

Matching Clothes

Underneath each picture, write the English word that matches the Spanish and the pictures. Write the Spanish words next to the English words at the bottom of the page.

pantalones cortos		cinturón	
vestido		botas	
chaqueta		blusa	
camisa			

1. belt _____

2. jacket _____

3. shirt _____

4. dress _____

5. boots _____

6. blouse _____

7. shorts _____

Nombre_____

Clothes Closet

Circle the Spanish words that you find in the puzzle. Write the English meanings at the bottom of the page next to the Spanish words from the puzzle.

v	s	q	o	d	i	t	s	e	v	f	a	o
i	e	a	c	o	y	f	f	n	a	s	g	g
r	n	b	t	j	n	c	l	l	e	i	j	u
x	ó	x	s	o	r	a	d	n	r	q	r	a
s	r	h	u	e	b	a	i	b	l	y	i	n
a	u	t	g	c	n	t	a	l	p	g	b	t
i	t	c	y	g	e	o	a	g	n	z	o	e
l	n	o	m	c	b	o	l	s	o	m	s	s
a	i	v	l	l	k	o	v	a	i	r	x	v
d	c	a	u	e	m	l	n	s	t	m	r	a
n	c	s	z	a	p	a	t	o	s	n	a	a
a	a	k	a	t	e	u	q	a	h	c	a	c
s	g	u	f	a	t	e	z	i	m	a	c	p

Spanish Word	English		Spanish Word	English
abrigo	_____		sandalias	_____
guantes	_____		calcetines	_____
blusa	_____		falda	_____
chaqueta	_____		vestido	_____
pantalones	_____		camisa	_____
botas	_____		gorra	_____
cinturón	_____		zapatos	_____

Face

ojos

nariz

orejas

dientes

Nombre_____

Face

cara

boca

pelo

Nombre_____

What's on Your Face?

Say each word out loud. Copy each word.

_____   _____
- - - - - - - - - - - - - - -   - - - - - - - - - - - - - - -
_____   _____

> pelo   > nariz

_____   _____
- - - - - - - - - - - - - - -   - - - - - - - - - - - - - - -
_____   _____

> ojos   > orejas

> dientes   > boca

_____   _____
- - - - - - - - - - - - - - -   - - - - - - - - - - - - - - -
_____   _____

> cara

- - - - - - - - - - - - - - -
_____

Which part of your face do you like the best? _____

(Answer in Spanish.)

Nombre_____

Face Riddles

Can you guess the answers to the following riddles? Use the size and shape of the letter blocks to write the Spanish word. Use the Word Bank at the bottom of the page.

There are two of me. Sometimes I need glasses. What am I?

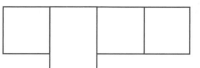

I like to be washed and combed. What am I?

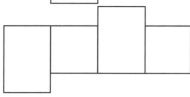

I help hold up glasses. When I feel an itch, I sneeze. What am I?

Everyone's looks a little different, in spite of the shape. What am I?

We grow, get loose, fall out, and grow again. What are we?

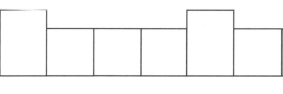

"Open wide" is often said when I am too small. What am I?

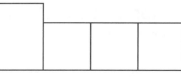

Does your mom always tell you to wash behind us? What are we?

nariz	pelo	dientes
ojos	orejas	cara	boca

Nombre_____

A Blank Face

Fill in the blanks with the missing letters. Use the Spanish words below to help you.

nariz   pelo   dientes   ojos   orejas   cara   boca

Which word didn't you use? _____

Color each block that has a letter k inside. Do not color the blocks with numbers. What hidden word did you find? _____

k	5	5	5	5	5	5	5	5	5	5	5	5	5	5	5
k	5	5	5	5	5	5	5	5	5	5	5	5	5	5	5
k	5	5	5	5	5	5	5	5	5	5	5	5	5	5	5
k	k	k	5	k	k	k	5	k	k	k	5	k	k	k	5
k	5	k	5	k	5	k	5	k	5	5	5	k	5	k	5
k	5	k	5	k	5	k	5	k	5	5	5	k	5	k	5
k	k	k	5	k	5	k	5	k	k	k	5	k	k	k	k

Head to Toe

Using the Word Banks, label the parts of the face and body.

Word Bank

cara   ojos   boca   nariz   dientes   orejas   pelo

Word Bank

cuerpo   cabeza   mano   pierna   hombro
brazo   dedo   pie   rodilla   estómago

Diagonal Digits

Circle the Spanish words you find in the word search. Then, write the English meanings next to the Spanish words at the bottom of the page.

o	o	b	o	j	o	s	y	f	g	e	r	k	a	z
v	r	p	o	t	k	k	z	m	t	b	s	i	p	a
y	z	e	r	c	e	g	b	i	a	q	z	c	n	n
w	j	p	j	e	a	h	w	s	h	c	q	r	a	i
v	z	e	q	a	u	l	g	d	k	d	e	r	a	s
j	r	l	a	x	s	c	t	s	b	i	i	r	e	d
o	g	o	f	f	v	j	e	h	p	z	a	t	p	m
k	o	i	y	g	r	u	f	s	o	c	n	v	v	w
a	d	h	z	x	r	e	w	r	t	e	p	t	b	m
l	o	f	g	b	k	z	b	a	i	ó	o	n	i	w
l	x	p	h	k	r	m	z	d	w	b	m	d	e	n
i	o	j	n	n	o	e	u	f	n	x	r	a	e	v
d	n	f	a	h	b	f	h	s	k	j	e	a	g	d
o	a	f	l	a	a	m	y	b	i	j	x	c	z	o
r	m	i	c	f	v	e	p	e	d	n	n	g	p	o

cara _____ nariz _____

cuerpo _____ pierna _____

brazo _____ rodilla _____

ojos _____ dientes _____

cabeza _____ hombro _____

dedo _____ estómago _____

boca _____ orejas _____

mano _____ pelo _____

Nombre_____

Head and Shoulders

Refer to the Word Bank to label each body part in Spanish.

Word Bank

cuerpo	pie
brazo	pierna
cabeza	rodilla
dedo	hombro
mano	estómago

Nombre_____

Knees and Toes

Write the Spanish words for the clues in the crossword puzzle.

Word Bank

cuerpo	cabeza	mano	pierna	hombro
brazo	dedo	pie	rodilla	estómago

Across
2. foot
3. body
5. knee
6. head
7. shoulder
9. hand

Down
1. finger or toe
2. leg
4. stomach
8. arm

Nombre_____

How Are You?

Label each facial feature with a Spanish word from the Word Bank.

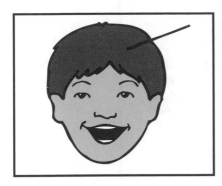 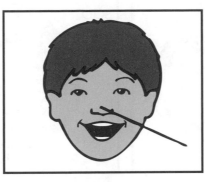 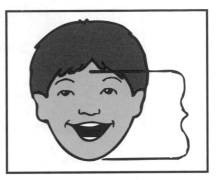

_____   _____   _____

  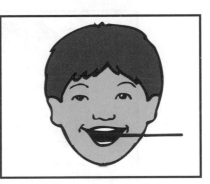

_____   _____   _____

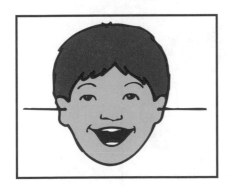

_____

Word Bank

cara	pelo
ojos	dientes
boca	orejas
nariz	

How Are You?

Copy the Spanish word that matches each face pictured.

happy

feliz

_____

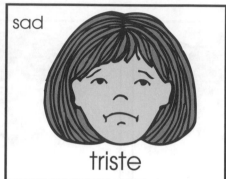

sad

triste

_____

smiling

sonriendo

_____

angry

enojada

_____

crying

llorando

_____

thinking

pensando

_____

Nombre_____

Happy or Sad?

Write the Spanish for the clue words in the crossword puzzle.

Across

1. sad
2. eyes
3. thinking
5. face
10. smiling
11. crying

Down

4. angry
6. teeth
7. ears
8. mouth
9. hair

Word Bank

llorando	orejas	sonriendo	ojos
pelo	pensando	triste	cara
dientes	boca	enojado	

Family

padre

madre

hermano

Nombre_____

Family

hermana

abuela

abuelo

Nombre_____

Family Words

Say each family word out loud.

| madre |  | mother |

| padre |  | father |

| hermana | | sister |

| hermano | | brother |

| abuela |  | grandmother |

| abuelo |  | grandfather |

Nombre_____

My Family

Draw a picture of your family. Color your picture.

Mi familia

Write the correct Spanish word next to each person in your picture above.

padre	abuelo	hermana
hermano	madre	abuela

Nombre_____

Family Word Meanings

Say each word out loud. Circle the picture that shows the meaning of each word.

| padre |  | |

| hermana | | |

| abuela |  |  |

| madre |  | |

| abuelo | |  |

| hermano | |  |

Nombre_____

Matching Family

Cut out a picture of a family out of a magazine. Glue each picture next to the correct word.

 padre ☐

 hermana ☐

 madre ☐

abuelo ☐

hermano ☐

 abuela ☐

Color each block with a letter inside. Do not color the blocks with numbers. What hidden word did you find? _____

2	2	2	2	2	2	2	2	2	2	2	2	2	m	2	2	2	2	2	2	2
2	2	2	2	2	2	2	2	2	2	2	2	2	m	2	2	2	2	2	2	2
m	m	m	m	m	2	m	m	m	2	2	m	m	m	2	m	m	m	2	m	m	m
m	2	m	2	m	2	m	2	m	2	2	m	2	m	2	m	2	m	2	m	2	m
m	2	m	2	m	2	m	2	m	2	2	m	2	m	2	m	2	2	2	m	m	m
m	2	m	2	m	2	m	2	m	2	2	m	2	m	2	m	2	2	2	m	2	2
m	2	m	2	m	2	m	m	m	m	2	m	m	m	2	m	2	2	2	m	m	m

Nombre_____

Family

Copy each word and color the pictures.

_____
- - - - - - - - - - - - -
_____

> madre

_____
- - - - - - - - - - - - -
_____

> padre

_____
- - - - - - - - - - - - -
_____

> abuelo

_____
- - - - - - - - - - - - -
_____

> abuela

_____
- - - - - - - - - - - - -
_____

> hermana

_____
- - - - - - - - - - - - -
_____

> hermano

Let's learn two
new words:

boy

_____
- - - - - - - - - - - - -
_____

> chico

girl

_____
- - - - - - - - - - - - -
_____

> chica

Nombre_____

Family Crossword

Use the Spanish words at the bottom of the page to fill in your answers.

ACROSS
1. sister
4. father
5. mother
6. girl
7. boy

DOWN
1. brother
2. grandmother
3. grandfather

padre	madre
chico	chica
abuelo	abuela
hermano	hermana

Nombre_____

Listen Well

Say each word out loud. Circle the picture for each Spanish word.

padre			
abuelo			
hermana			
chica			
abuela			
madre			
hermano			
chico			

Nombre_____

Family Ties

In each box, copy the Spanish word for family members.

la familia	el padre
family	father
la madre	el hijo
mother	son
la hija	los primos
daughter	cousins

Write the Spanish words from above next to the English words.

family _____   mother _____

cousins _____   daughter _____

father _____   son _____

Nombre_____

Family Ties

In each box, copy the Spanish word for family members.

el hermano	la hermana
brother	sister
el tío	la tía
uncle	aunt
el abuelo	la abuela
grandfather	grandmother

Write the Spanish words from above next to the English words.

sister _____   uncle _____

grandfather _____   brother _____

grandmother _____   aunt _____

Nombre_____

My Family

Write the Spanish word for each clue in the crossword puzzle.

Across

2. son
3. aunt
5. sister
7. grandmother
8. brother
10. cousins

Down

1. mother
2. daughter
4. family
6. grandfather
9. uncle
10. father

Word Bank

familia	hermano	hijo	tía
primos	madre	tío	abuelo
padre	hermana	hija	abuela

Nombre_____

Family Tree

Refer to the Word Bank to write the Spanish word that matches each picture.

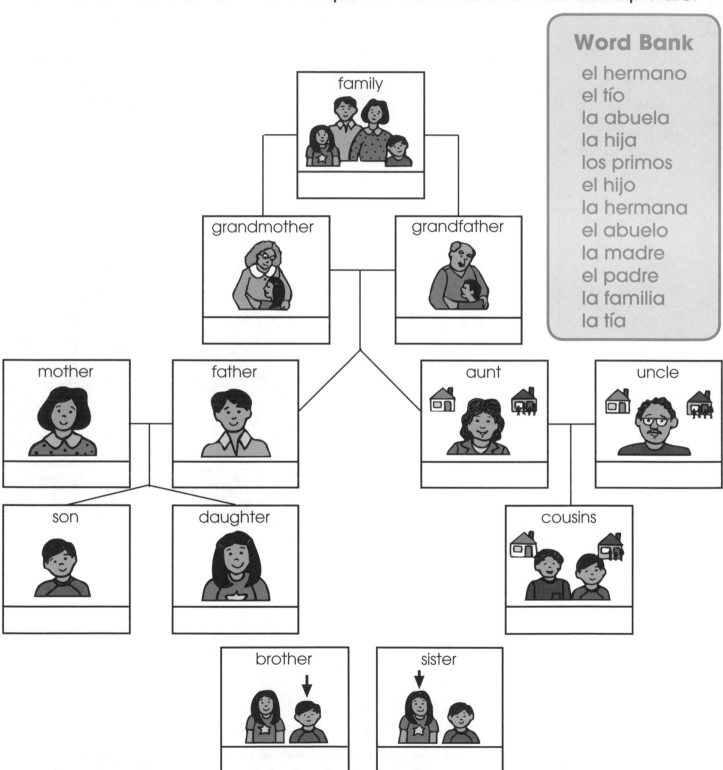

Word Bank

el hermano
el tío
la abuela
la hija
los primos
el hijo
la hermana
el abuelo
la madre
el padre
la familia
la tía

Relationships

How are the following people related? Read the Spanish sentences carefully. Use the words in the Word Bank to complete each sentence. You may use each word only once, and some words may not be used at all. Then, write the English meaning of each sentence on the line below the sentence.

Word Bank

hermano   hija   hermana   padre   tío   primos
abuela   abuelo   familia   hijo   madre   tía

1. La madre de mi madre es mi _____ .
_____

2. Los hijos de mi tío son mis _____ .
_____

3. La hija de mi madre es mi _____ .
_____

4. El hermano de mi padre es mi _____ .
_____

5. El padre de mi padre es mi _____ .
_____

6. Mi tío es el hermano di mi _____ .
_____

7. La hermana de mi madre es mi _____ .
_____

8. La hermana de mi tía es mi _____ .
_____

Nombre_____

Community

biblioteca

escuela

parque

Nombre_____

Community

tienda

casa

museo

Places to Go

Say the Spanish words out loud.

| escuela |  | school |

| museo |  | museum |

| casa |  | house |

| tienda |  | store |

| biblioteca |  | library |

| parque |  | park |

Picture This

Say each word out loud. Circle the picture that shows the meaning of each word.

casa

escuela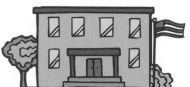

tienda

parque

biblioteca

museo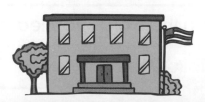

My Neighborhood

Draw a picture of a neighborhood. Draw places you have learned about in this book. Add streets, trees, and whatever else you wish to make your neighborhood look nice. Color your picture.

Mi barrio

Label your neighborhood with the words you learned.

| casa | parque | biblioteca | tienda | escuela | museo |

Nombre_____

Places, Please

Cut out pictures that match the words below. Glue each picture next to the correct word.

casa		tienda	

parque		escuela	

biblioteca		museo	

Color each block with a letter Y inside. Do not color the blocks with numbers. What hidden word did you find? _____

q	q	q	q	q	q	q	q	q	q	q	q	q	q	q	q	q	q
y	y	y	q	y	y	y	q	q	y	y	y	q	y	y	y	y	q
y	q	y	q	y	q	y	q	q	y	q	q	q	y	q	y	q	q
y	q	q	q	y	q	y	q	q	y	y	y	q	y	q	y	q	q
y	q	y	q	y	q	y	q	q	q	q	y	q	y	q	y	q	q
y	y	y	q	y	y	y	y	q	y	y	y	q	y	y	y	y	y
q	q	q	q	q	q	q	q	q	q	q	q	q	q	q	q	q	q

Nombre_____

Places to Go

Say each word out loud. Copy each word and color the picture.

> museo

> escuela

> casa

> tienda

> biblioteca

> parque

Nombre_____

A Place for Riddles

Answer the riddles. Use the size and shape of the letter blocks to write the Spanish words. The answers at the bottom of the page will help you.

People live in me. What am I?

If you want to buy something, you come to me. What am I?

People like to come to me for playing and relaxing. What am I?

I am filled with books that you can borrow. What am I?

I am filled with children, desks, and books. What am I?

I often have dinosaur bones. What am I?

escuela   museo   casa
biblioteca   tienda   parque

Nombre_____

Our Town

Draw a picture of a town showing community places that you have learned. Label them in Spanish. Use the words at the bottom of the page.

escuela	museo	casa
biblioteca	tienda	parque

Nombre_____

Place Words

Fill in the blanks for place words. Use the Spanish words at the bottom of the page to help you.

b i b l i o t e c a

escuela   museo   casa
biblioteca   tienda   parque

Nombre_____

Where Am I?

On this page and the next page, refer to the Word Bank and write the Spanish word for each place in the community pictured.

movie theater

farm

church

park

apartment

restaurant

Word Bank

escuela	granja	biblioteca	tienda
museo	casa	apartamento	zoológico
iglesia	restaurante	cine	parque

Nombre_____

Where Am I?

museum

zoo

library

store

house

school

Word Bank

escuela	granja	biblioteca	tienda
museo	casa	apartamento	zoológico
iglesia	restaurante	cine	parque

Nombre_____

Fitting In

Write the Spanish words from the Word Bank in the word blocks. Write the English meanings below the blocks.

Word Bank

granja	casa
cine	iglesia
museo	parque
tienda	restaurante
escuela	biblioteca

1.
   _____

2.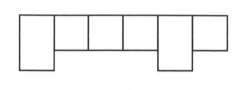
   _____

3.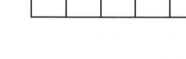
   _____

4.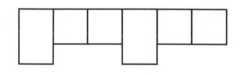
   _____

5.
   _____

6.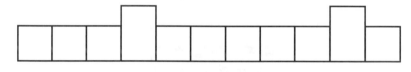
   _____

7.
   _____

8.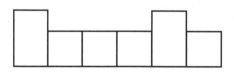
   _____

9.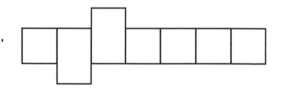
   _____

10.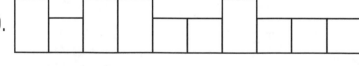
    _____

Name That Place

On your turn roll the die, move your marker, and say the name of the place in Spanish.

• If you can't remember a Spanish word, ask for help and skip a turn.

• The winner is the player to reach the finish first.

• For two to four players.

Around the House

Copy the Spanish words. Then, write the English words below them.

casa

_____

_____

cocina

_____

_____

sala

_____

_____

dormitorio

_____

_____

sofá

_____

_____

cama

_____

_____

lámpara

_____

_____

cuchara

_____

_____

Word Bank

couch	kitchen	lamp	spoon
bedroom	bed	house	living room

Nombre_____

Around the House

Write the Spanish words from the Word Bank that fit in these word blocks.
Write the English below the blocks.

> ## Word Bank
>
> casa   dormitorio   lámpara
> cocina   sofá   cuchara
> sala   cama

1.

2.

3.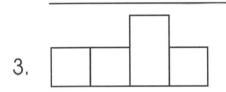

4.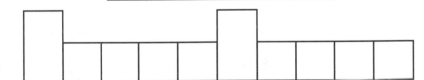

5.

6.

7.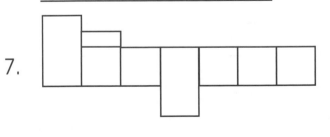

8.

A Blue House

Copy the sentences in Spanish on the first lines. Write the sentences in English on the second lines.

1. La casa es azul. _____

 _____

2. La sala es marrón. _____

 _____

3. El dormitorio es morado. _____

 _____

4. La cuchara es verde. _____

 _____

5. El sofá es rosado. _____

 _____

6. La cama es azul. _____

 _____

7. La lámpara es amarilla. _____

 _____

Challenge:

La fruta está en la cocina. _____

_____

_____

_____

Nombre_____

Around Town

Write the Spanish words to match the pictures. Write the English next to the Spanish at the bottom of the page.

park 	apartment 	restaurant 
school 	museum 	zoo 

house

1. escuela _____

2. casa _____

3. parque _____

4. museo _____

5. apartamento _____

6. restaurante _____

7. zoológico _____

Around Town

Write the Spanish words to match the pictures. Write the English next to the Spanish at the bottom of the page.

farm 	country 	city 
library 	church 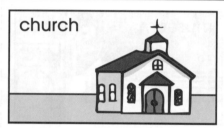	store 

movie theater

1. iglesia _____
2. biblioteca _____
3. tienda _____
4. cine _____

5. granja _____
6. ciudad _____
7. campo _____

Nombre_____

Up the Street

Circle the Spanish community related words that you find in the word search. Write the English beside the Spanish at the bottom of the page.

t	c	b	e	s	c	u	e	l	a	m	t	a
e	e	i	a	d	n	e	i	t	u	j	j	p
t	n	n	u	n	o	l	a	s	a	n	p	a
n	i	d	a	d	i	y	e	s	a	n	n	r
a	g	l	a	s	a	o	f	r	a	i	l	t
r	l	t	h	e	t	d	g	o	o	r	ñ	a
u	e	z	o	o	l	ó	g	i	c	o	n	m
a	s	q	p	u	i	l	i	c	i	k	b	e
t	i	p	m	a	j	l	o	f	n	o	r	n
s	a	m	a	s	u	x	o	n	e	w	r	t
e	e	d	c	a	e	u	q	r	a	p	e	o
r	o	v	a	c	e	t	o	i	l	b	i	b

Spanish Word   **English**

escuela _____

iglesia _____

zoológico _____

campo _____

casa _____

apartamento _____

museo _____

Spanish Word   **English**

tienda _____

biblioteca _____

ciudad _____

restaurante _____

granja _____

cine _____

parque _____

Home, Sweet Home

At the bottom of each picture, copy the Spanish word.

dormitorio

vaso

estufa

sala

baño

televisión

Write the Spanish word after each room or household item.

bathroom _____   living room _____

television _____   stove _____

bedroom _____   glass _____

Nombre_____

Home, Sweet Home

At the bottom of each picture, copy the Spanish word.

cocina

_____

casa

_____

lámpara

_____

toalla

_____

cama

_____

teléfono

_____

Write the Spanish word after each room or household item.

towel _____   bed _____

kitchen _____   telephone _____

lamp _____   house _____

Nombre_____

Around the House

Write the Spanish words for the clue words in the crossword puzzle.

Across

2. kitchen
3. lamp
5. towel
8. living room
9. telephone
11. stove

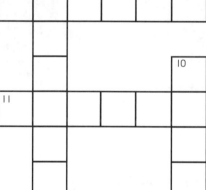

Down

1. bedroom
2. house
4. bed
6. television set
7. bathroom
10. glass

Word Bank

baño	cocina	lámpara	televisión
dormitorio	teléfono	toalla	cama
vaso	casa	estufa	sala

Nombre_____

Classroom Objects

libro

lápiz

tijeras

Nombre_____

Classroom Objects

borrador

mesa

silla

Nombre_____

Classroom Things

Say each word out loud.

| silla |  | chair |

| libro |  | book |

| mesa |  | table |

| lápiz | | pencil |

| tijeras |  | scissors |

| borrador | | eraser |

Nombre_____

Matching Objects

Draw a line from the word to the correct picture. Color the picture.

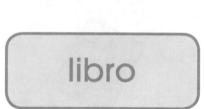

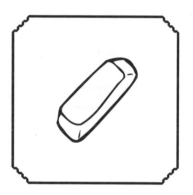

libro

mesa

lápiz

tijeras

borrador

Nombre_____

Draw and Color Your Classroom

Draw and color a picture for each word listed. Which ones do you have in your classroom? Circle them.

silla

libro

mesa

lápiz

tijeras

borrador

Nombre_____

Match Words and Pictures

Cut out pictures from a magazine and glue each picture next to the correct word.

silla	

borrador	

mesa	

Nombre_____

Match Words and Pictures

Cut out pictures from a magazine and glue each picture next to the correct word.

lápiz	

tijeras	

libro	

Nombre_____

Classroom Things

Copy each word and color the picture.

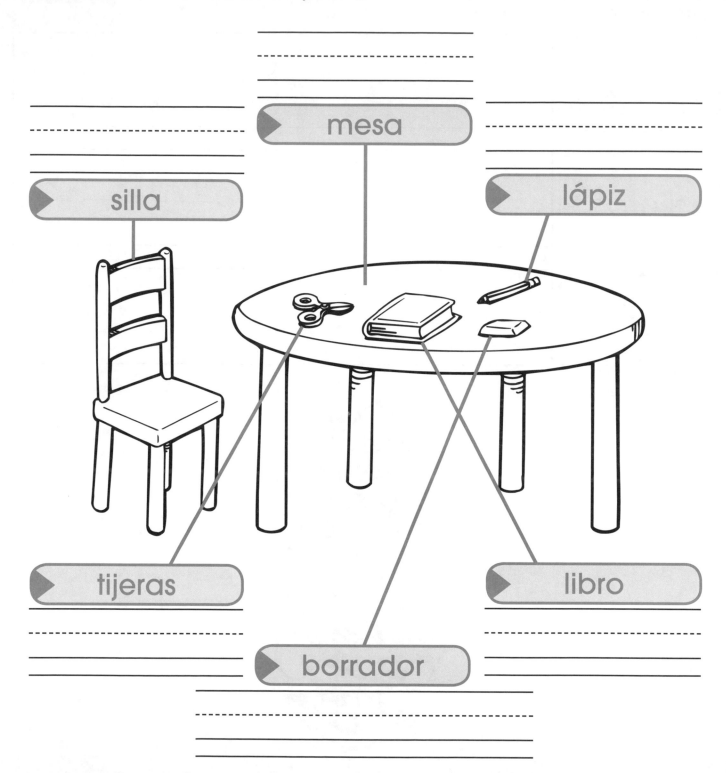

mesa

silla

lápiz

tijeras

libro

borrador

Nombre_____

New Classroom Words

Say each word out loud. Copy each word and color the picture.

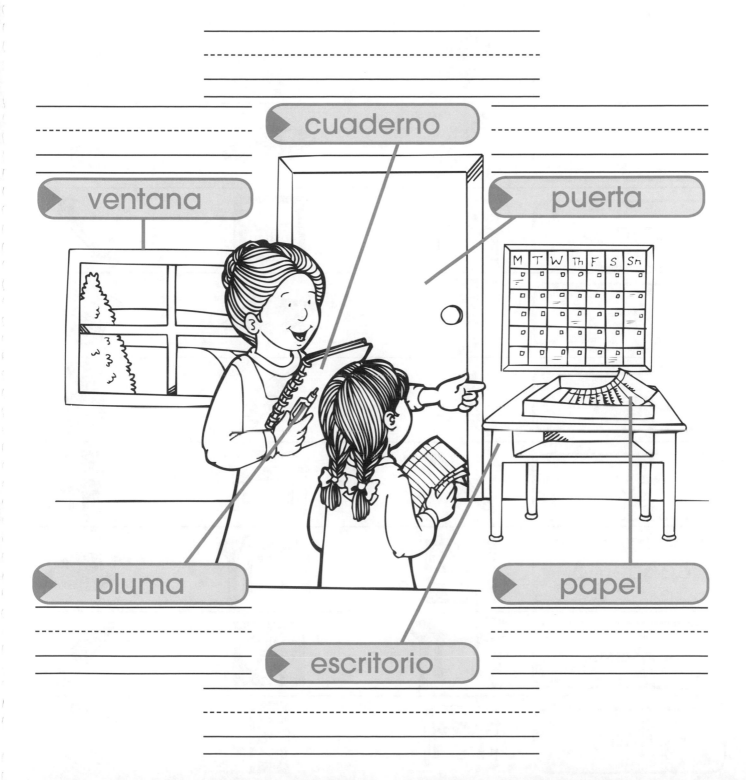

cuaderno

ventana

puerta

pluma

papel

escritorio

Listen Carefully

Say each word out loud. Circle the picture that tells the meaning of each word.

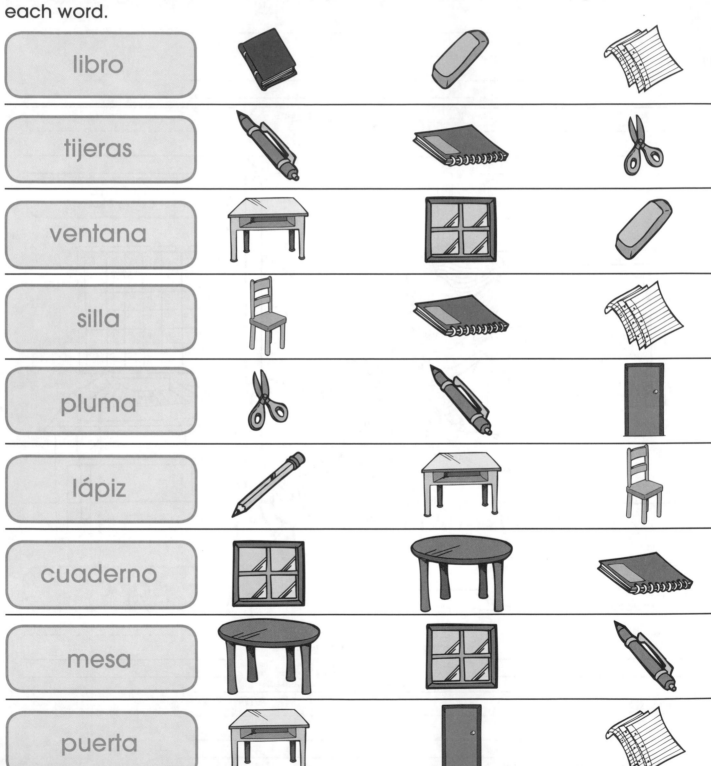

libro

tijeras

ventana

silla

pluma

lápiz

cuaderno

mesa

puerta

Use the Clues

Use the clues and the words at the bottom of the page. Do not use any answer more than once.

1. Both words begin with the letter *p*. You write <u>with</u> one and write <u>on</u> one. What are they?

   _____   _____

2. You can sit at either one of these when you need to write.

   _____   _____

3. You could exit through either one of these in case of fire.

   _____   _____

4. Both words end with the letter *o*. They both have pages.

   _____   _____

5. These two words go together because one is on the end of the other.

   _____   _____

6. Both words have an *i* as their second letter. One is used for cutting and the other is used for sitting.

   _____   _____

silla	mesa	tijeras	libro	borrador	ventana
puerta	lápiz	cuaderno	papel	escritorio	pluma

Nombre_____

Around the Room

In each box, copy the Spanish word for the classroom object pictured.

silla		lápiz	
puerta		papel	
ventana		escritorio	

Write the Spanish words from above next to the English words.

window _____   chair _____

desk _____   door _____

paper _____   pencil _____

Nombre_____

Around the Room

In each box, copy the Spanish word for the classroom object pictured.

mesa	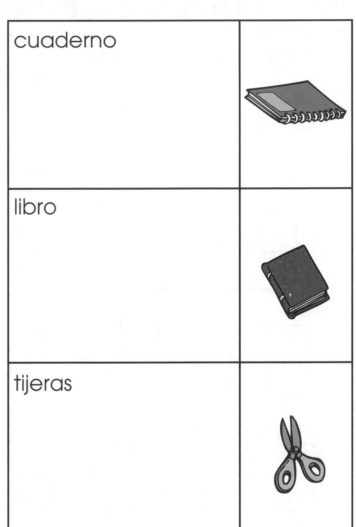	cuaderno	
pluma		libro	
borrador		tijeras	

Write the Spanish words from above next to the English words.

eraser _____   book _____

scissors _____   table _____

pen _____   notebook _____

Nombre_____

A Fitting Design

Write the Spanish words from the Word Bank that fit in these word blocks. Write the English meanings below the blocks.

1.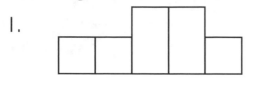

2.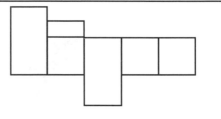

3.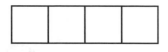

4.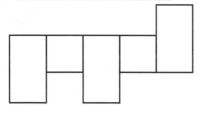

5.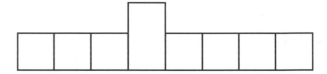

6.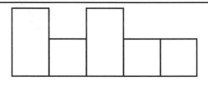

7.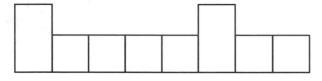

8.

9.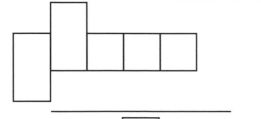

10.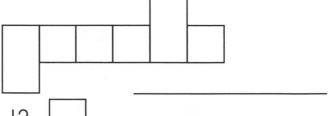

11.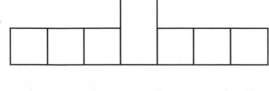

12.

Nombre_____

Where's My Pencil?

Circle the Spanish words that you find in the word search. Then, write the English meaning of each word.

w	p	p	a	r	t	m	a	m	u	l	p
r	u	x	f	s	o	t	r	h	h	o	n
x	e	d	e	j	e	d	j	j	i	m	l
o	r	a	h	v	z	m	a	r	a	o	u
o	t	o	f	e	i	f	o	r	m	i	l
n	a	r	t	s	e	t	s	l	r	y	o
r	p	b	f	p	i	a	m	l	h	o	v
e	i	i	g	r	r	e	p	n	d	m	b
d	w	l	c	e	y	e	a	l	l	i	s
a	q	s	j	l	e	f	l	e	p	a	p
u	e	i	l	a	p	i	z	i	m	t	d
c	t	v	e	n	t	a	n	a	i	n	i

Spanish Word	English	Spanish Word	English
ventana	_____	pluma	_____
borrador	_____	libro	_____
escritorio	_____	mesa	_____
papel	_____	puerta	_____
silla	_____	cuaderno	_____
tijeras	_____	lápiz	_____

Nombre_____

Classroom Clutter

Draw a picture to illustrate each of the Spanish words. Refer to the Word Bank at the bottom of the page to help you.

silla	mesa
tijeras	libro
lápiz	borrador

Word Bank

eraser	chair	scissors	pencil	book	table

Nombre_____

Classroom Clutter

Draw a picture to illustrate each of the Spanish words. Refer to the Word Bank at the bottom of the page to help you.

ventana	puerta
papel	cuaderno
escritorio	pluma

Word Bank

door   notebook   pen   desk   window   paper

Nombre_____

Show and Tell

Write the Spanish word for each clue in the crossword puzzle.

Across

1. notebook
5. scissors
7. pen
8. eraser
10. pencil
11. table
12. chair

Down

2. desk
3. window
4. book
6. door
9. paper

Word Bank

escritorio	mesa	libro	silla	tijeras	puerta
lápiz	ventana	borrador	cuaderno	papel	pluma

Nombre_____

Pencil and Paper

Copy the following sentences in Spanish. Then, write the English meanings.

1. El libro es rojo. _____

_____

2. La silla es marrón. _____

_____

3. El cuaderno es morado. _____

_____

4. La mesa es verde. _____

_____

5. El lápiz es rosado. _____

_____

Nombre_____

Pencil and Paper

Copy the following sentences in Spanish. Then, write the English meanings.

6. El borrador es amarillo. _____

_____

7. La ventana es azul. _____

_____

8. El escritorio es anaranjado. _____

_____

9. El papel es blanco. _____

_____

Nombre_____

Songs and Chants

Diez (veinte) amigos
(to the tune of "Ten Little Fingers")

Uno, dos, tres amigos,
cuatro, cinco, seis amigos,
siete, ocho, nueve amigos,
diez amigos son.

Diez, nueve, ocho amigos
siete, seis, cinco amigos
cuatro, tres, dos amigos,
un amigo es.

Once, doce, trece amigos,
catorce, quince, dieciséis amigos,
diecisiete, dieciocho,
diecinueve amigos,
veinte amigos son.

Community Song
(to the tune of "Here We Go 'Round the Mulberry Bush")

Escuela is school,
museo — museum,
casa is house,
tienda is store,
biblioteca is library,
parque is the park for me!

Songs and Chants

Family Song
(to the tune of "Are You Sleeping?")

Padre — father,
madre — mother,
chico — boy,
chica — girl,
abuelo is grandpa,
abuela is grandma.
Our family, our family.

Hermano — brother,
hermana — sister,
chico — boy,
chica — girl,
padre y madre,
abuelo y abuela.
Our family, our family.

Los días de la semana
(to the tune of "Clementine")

Domingo, lunes,
martes, miércoles,
jueves, viernes, sábado,
domingo, lunes,
martes, miércoles,
jueves, viernes, sábado.
(Repitan)

Nombre_____

Songs and Chants

¡Hola! Means Hello
(to the tune of "London Bridge")

¡Hola! means hello-o-o, hello-o-o, hello-o-o.
¡Hola! means hello-o-o. ¡Hola, amigos!

¡Adiós! Means Good-bye
(to the tune of "London Bridge")

¡Adiós! means goo-ood-bye, goo-ood-bye, goo-ood-bye.
¡Adiós! means goo-ood-bye. ¡Adiós, amigos!

Cinco amigos
(to the tune of "Ten Little Fingers")

Uno, dos, tres, cuatro, cinco,
Uno, dos, tres, cuatro, cinco,
Uno, dos, tres, cuatro, cinco,
Cinco amigos son.

Songs and Chants

Diez amigos
(to the tune of "Ten Little Fingers")

Uno, dos, tres amigos,
cuatro, cinco, seis amigos,
siete, ocho, nueve amigos,
diez amigos son.

Diez, nueve, ocho amigos,
siete, seis, cinco amigos,
cuatro, tres, dos amigos,
un amigo es.

Colors Song
(to the tune of "Twinke, Twinkle Little Star")

Red is rojo,
purple, morado,
yellow, amarillo,
pink is rosado,
white is blanco,
colors, colores,

green is verde,
brown, marrón;
blue, azul,
orange, anaranjado;
black is negro,
colors, colores.

Songs and Chants

Classroom Objects Song
(to the tune of "The Farmer in the Dell")

A silla is a chair;
A libro is a book;
A mesa is a table in our classroom.

A lápiz is a pencil;
Tijeras are scissors;
A borrador is an eraser in our classroom.

Clothing Song
(to the tune of "Skip to My Lou")

Camisa — shirt,   pantalones — pants,
vestido — dress,   calcetines — socks,
zapatos — shoes, gorra — cap
These are the clothes that we wear.

Songs and Chants

Food Song
(to the tune of "She'll Be Coming 'Round the Mountain")

Queso is cheese, yum, yum, yum. (clap, clap)
Leche is milk, yum, yum, yum. (clap, clap)
Papa is potato.
Jugo is juice.
Pan is bread, yum, yum, yum! (clap, clap)

Pollo is chicken, yum, yum, yum. (clap, clap)
Ensalada is salad, yum, yum, yum. (clap, clap)
Queso, leche, papa,
jugo, pan, pollo, ensalada,
yum, yum, yum, yum, yum! (clap, clap)

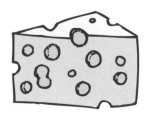  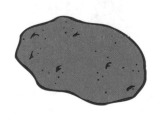 

Songs and Chants

Name Chant
(snap, clap, snap, clap with the rhythm
 of the question and answer)

Teacher: *¿Cómo te llamas?*

Student: *Me llamo* _____.
(Repeat until everyone has had a turn
answering the question.)

Adiós Means Good-bye
(to the tune of "London Bridge")

Adiós means goo-ood-bye,
        goo-ood-bye,
        goo-ood-bye.
Adiós means goo-ood-bye.
¡Adiós, amigos!

¡Hasta luego! — see you later,
        see you later,
        see you later.
¡Hasta luego! — see you later.

¡Hasta luego, amigos!

Diez (veinte) amigos
(to the tune of "Ten Little Fingers")

*Uno, dos, tres amigos,
cuatro, cinco, seis amigos,
siete, ocho, nueve amigos,
diez amigos son.*

*Diez, nueve, ocho amigos
siete, seis, cinco amigos
cuatro, tres, dos amigos,
un amigo es.*

*Once, doce, trece amigos,
catorce, quince, dieciséis amigos,
diecisiete, dieciocho,
diecinueve amigos,
veinte amigos son.*

Nombre_____

Songs and Chants

Classroom Objects Song
(to the tune of "The Farmer in the Dell")

A *silla* is a chair,
a *libro* is a book,
a *mesa* is a table in our classroom.

A *lápiz* is a pencil,
tijeras are scissors,
a *borrador* is an eraser in our classroom.

Ventana is a window,
cuaderno is a notebook,
papel is paper in our classroom.

A *puerta* is a door,
a *pluma* is a pen,
escritorio is a desk in our classroom.

Food Song
(to the tune of "She'll Be Coming 'Round the Mountain")

Part 1
Queso is cheese, yum, yum, yum
(clap, clap)
leche is milk, yum, yum, yum
(clap, clap)
papa is potato, *jugo* is juice,
pan is bread,
yum, yum, yum! (clap, clap)

Pollo is chicken, yum, yum, yum
(clap, clap)
ensalada is salad, yum, yum, yum
(clap, clap)
queso, leche, papa, jugo, pan,
pollo, ensalada,
yum, yum, yum, yum, yum!
(clap, clap)

Face Song
(to the tune of "Here We Go 'Round the Mulberry Bush")

Ojos — eyes, *boca* — mouth,
nariz — nose, *dientes* — teeth,
orejas — ears, *pelo* — hair,
cara is my face.

Part 2
Sándwich is sandwich, yum, yum, yum
(clap, clap)
manzana is apple, yum, yum, yum
(clap, clap)
sopa is soup, *agua* is water,
carne is meat,
yum, yum, yum! (clap, clap)

Naranja is orange, yum, yum, yum
(clap, clap)
plátano is banana, yum, yum, yum
(clap, clap)
sándwich, manzana, sopa, agua,
carne, naranja, plátano,
yum, yum, yum, yum, yum!
(clap, clap)

Nombre_____

Songs and Chants

Animals Song
(to the tune of "This Old Man")

Gato — cat,
perro — dog,
pájaro is a flying bird,
pez is a fish, and
pato is a duck,
culebra is a slinky snake.

Clothing Song
(to the tune of "Skip to My Lou")

Camisa — shirt, *pantalones* — pants,
vestido — dress, *calcetines* — socks,
zapatos — shoes, *gorra* — cap.
These are the clothes that we wear.

Chaqueta — jacket, *botas* — boots,
abrigo — dress, *falda* — skirt,
guantes are gloves. What did we forget?
Pantalones cortos are shorts.

Songs and Chants

Alphabet Song
(to the tune of "B-I-N-G-O")

A	**B**	**C**	**D**	**E**	**F**	**G**
(There	was	a	farmer	had	a	dog)

H	**I**	**J**	**K**
(and Bin-	go	was his	name-o.)

L	**M**	**N**	**—**	**O**
(B	I	N	G	O)

P	**Q**	**R**	**S**	**T**
(B	I	N	G	O)

U	**V**	**W**
(B	I	N G O)

X	**Y**		**Z**
(and	Bingo was his		name-o.)

Songs

¡Hola, chicos!
(to the tune of "Goodnight Ladies")

¡Hola, chico! ¡Hola, chica!
¡Hola, chicos! ¿Cómo están hoy?
¡Hola, chico! ¡Hola, chica!
¡Hola, chicos! ¿Cómo están hoy?

Songs

Cumpleaños feliz
(to the tune of "Happy Birthday")

Cumpleaños feliz,
Cumpleaños feliz,
Te deseamos a ti,
Cumpleaños feliz.

Así me lavo las manos
(to the tune of "Here We Go Round the Mulberry Bush")

Así me lavo las manos, las manos, las manos

(Use hand motions to show hand washing.)

Así me lavo las manos, por la mañana.
Así me lavo la cara, la cara, la cara

(Use hand motions to show face washing.)

Así me lavo la cara, por la mañana.
Así me lavo los pies, los pies, los pies

(Use different body parts that students pick.)

(los brazos, el estómago, etc.)

Songs

Fray Felipe
(to the tune of "Are You Sleeping?")

Fray Felipe, Fray Felipe, ¿Duermes tú, duermes tú?
Toca la campana, toca la campana, tan, tan, tan, tan, tan, tan.

Fray Francisco, Fray Francisco, ¿Duermes tú, duermes tú?
Toca la campana, toca la campana, tan, tan, tan, tan, tan, tan.

Christmas Carols

Cascabeles
("Jingle Bells")

O, que felicidad caminar en un trineo
por los caminos que blancos ya están.
Nos paseamos con gritos de alegría,
con cantos y risas de dicha caminamos.
O, cascabeles, cascabeles, tra la la la la,
qué alegría todo el día, tra la la la la.
Cascabeles, cascabeles, tra la la la la,
qué alegría todo el día, tra la la la la.

Noche de paz
("Silent Night")

Noche de paz, noche de amor,
todo duerme en derredor.
Entre los astros que esparcen la luz,
bella anunciando al niño Jesús.
Brilla la estrella de paz,
Brilla la estrella de paz.
Noche de paz, noche de amor,
oye humilde el fiel pastor.
Coros celestes que anuncian salud,
gracias y glorias en gran plenitud.
Por nuestro buen Redentor,
Por nuestro buen Redentor.

Christmas Carols

Pueblecito de Belén
("Oh, Little Town of Bethlehem")

O, pueblecito de Belén, la cuna de Jesús,
bendito pueblo de Belén, la cuna de Jesús.
El Rey tan adorado, el santo Redentor,
el Rey que vino al mundo, a darnos paz y amor.

Chants

Body Chant
Cabeza, hombros, rodillas, dedos, rodillas, dedos, rodillas, dedos
Cabeza, hombros, rodillas, dedos
Ojos, orejas, boca, nariz.

Clothing Chant
Abrigo rosado, vestido blanco,
camisa marrón, sombrero morado,
blusas verdes, pantalones rojos,
botas azules, zapatos negros.

Pink coat, white dress,
brown shirt, purple hat,
green blouses, red pants,
blue boots, black shoes.

Adjective Chant
La casa es grande, la mesa—pequeña,

la puerta—cerrada, la ventana abierta.

The house is big,
the table—small,
the door—closed,
the window—open.

Papa Chant
Yo como una papa, no como a mi papá.
    I eat a potato, I don't eat my dad.
Una papa es comida, un papá es un padre.
    A papa is a potato, a papá is a father.

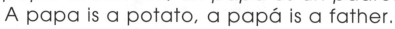

*Due to differences in
languages, literal translations
of chants may lose meaning
and/or the sense of rhythm.

Chants

The Pledge of Allegiance

Juro fidelidad a la bandera de los Estados Unidos de América, y a la república que representa, una nación bajo Dios, indivisible, con libertad y justicia para todos.

Vowel Chant

A, E, I, O, U *¡Más sabe el burro que tú!*

(A, E, I, O, U A donkey knows more than you!)

A, E, I, O, U *¿Cuántos años tienes tú?*

A, E, I, O, U How old are you?)

Number Chant

Dos y dos son cuatro, cuatro y dos son seis, seis, y dos son ocho, y ocho más, dieciséis.

(Two and two are four, four and two are six, six and two are eight, and eight more, sixteen)

Body Chant

Cabeza, hombros, rodillas y dedos, rodillas y dedos, rodillas y dedos
Cabeza, hombros, rodillas y dedos
Ojos, orejas, boca, y nariz.

*Due to differences in languages, literal translations of chants may lose meaning and/or the sense of rhythm.

Jack and the Beanstalk

Once upon a time, a poor widow lived with her son, Jack.

"Son," Jack's mother said, "We need money. You must take the cow to town and sell it."

Había un vez una viuda pobre que vivía con su hijo, Juan.

—Hijo, —dijo la mamá de Juan—. Necesitamos dinero. Tienes que llevar la vaca al pueblo y venderla.

Jack and the Beanstalk

Jack and the Beanstalk

Jack and the Beanstalk

Jack was halfway to town when a man stopped him.

"Jack," said the man, "I will give you five magic beans for your cow."

Jack traded the cow for the beans. He went home, very pleased with the deal.

Juan iba a mitad de camino hacia el pueblo cuando un hombre lo detuvo.

—Juan, —dijo el hombre—, te daré cinco frijoles mágicos a cambio de tu vaca.

Juan cambió la vaca por los frijoles, y se fue a casa muy complacido con el trato.

Jack and the Beanstalk

Jack's mother was not pleased.
"There are no such things as magic beans!" she cried.
Angrily, she threw the beans out the window.
"Now, we have no cow and no money!"

La mamá de Juan no estaba contenta.
—¡No existe tal cosa como frijoles mágicos! —gritó ella.
Enojada, tiró los frijoles por la ventana.
—Ahora, no tenemos ¡ni vaca ni dinero!

Jack and the Beanstalk

Jack and the Beanstalk

Nombre_____

Jack and the Beanstalk

When Jack woke the next morning, he looked out his window. A thick beanstalk stretched up to the clouds.

"They were magic beans," he whispered.

Without waking his mother, Jack climbed the beanstalk. At the top, he saw a castle.

A la mañana siguiente, cuando Juan se despertó, miró por la ventana. Un grueso tallo de frijoles subía hasta alcanzar las nubes.

—Eran frijoles mágicos, —susurró.

Sin despertar a su mamá, Juan se trepó por el tallo. En la cúspide, vio un castillo.

Jack and the Beanstalk

Jack and the Beanstalk

Jack knocked on the castle door. A giant woman opened it.
"Do you have any work I can do for food?" asked Jack.
Thud! Thud! Thud!
"It is my husband. Hide so he does not eat you."

Juan llamó a la puerta del castillo y una mujer gigante le abrió.
—¿Tiene algún trabajo que yo pueda hacer a cambio de comida?
—preguntó Juan.
¡Cataplum! ¡Cataplum! ¡Cataplum!
—Es mi esposo. Escóndete para que no te coma.

Jack and the Beanstalk

Jack and the Beanstalk

The giant came in. He said, "Fee, fi, foe, fum! I smell the blood of an Englishman!"

"Do not be silly," his wife said. "You smell breakfast."

After he ate, the giant began counting his gold. He soon fell asleep.

El gigante entró y dijo, —¡Ummm! ¡Ñam! ¡Ñam! ¡Huelo la sangre de un inglés!

—No seas tonto, —dijo su esposa—. Lo que hueles es el desayuno.

Después de comer, el gigante comenzó a contar sus monedas de oro. Pronto se quedó dormido.

Jack and the Beanstalk

Just a little gold would feed mother and me for a long time, Jack thought. He snatched a small bag and climbed down the beanstalk.

«Solo unas cuantas monedas de oro nos daría de comer a mi madre y a mi por mucho tiempo», —pensó Juan. Tomó una pequeña bolsa y bajó por el tallo de frijoles.

Jack and the Beanstalk

Jack told his mother where he got the gold.
She said, "Those giants robbed us of that gold
and two treasures. They killed your father."

Juan le contó a su mamá dónde había
conseguido las monedas de oro.
—Esos gigantes nos robaron ese oro y dos tesoros,
—dijo ella—. Ellos mataron a tu padre.

Jack and the Beanstalk

The next morning, Jack climbed the beanstalk again. He banged on the castle door. The giant woman peered down at him.
"Are you the thief who was here yesterday?" she demanded.

A la mañana siguiente, Juan trepó el tallo de frijoles nuevamente y tocó a la puerta del castillo. La mujer gigante lo escudriñó.
—¿Eres tú el ladrón que estuvo ayer aquí? —preguntó.

Jack and the Beanstalk

Jack and the Beanstalk

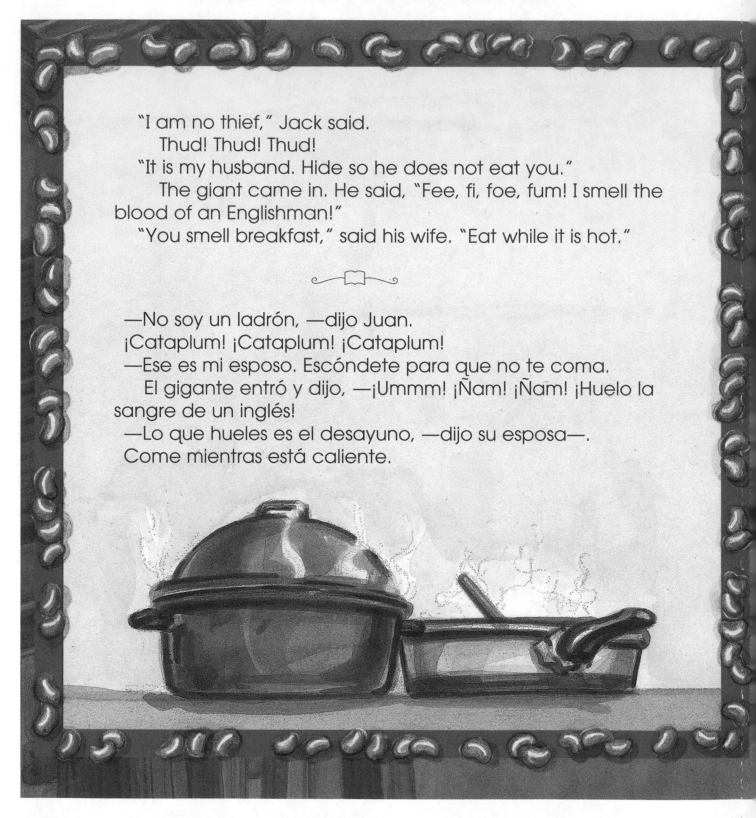

"I am no thief," Jack said.

Thud! Thud! Thud!

"It is my husband. Hide so he does not eat you."

The giant came in. He said, "Fee, fi, foe, fum! I smell the blood of an Englishman!"

"You smell breakfast," said his wife. "Eat while it is hot."

—No soy un ladrón, —dijo Juan.

¡Cataplum! ¡Cataplum! ¡Cataplum!

—Ese es mi esposo. Escóndete para que no te coma.

El gigante entró y dijo, —¡Ummm! ¡Ñam! ¡Ñam! ¡Huelo la sangre de un inglés!

—Lo que hueles es el desayuno, —dijo su esposa—.
Come mientras está caliente.

Jack and the Beanstalk

Jack and the Beanstalk

After he ate, the giant brought out a goose.
"Lay!" the giant roared.

The goose laid a golden egg on the table. The giant's eyes began to hurt from looking at the shiny gold. So, he shut them.

Después de comer, el gigante sacó un ganso.
—¡Pon un huevo! —rugió el gigante.

El ganso puso un huevo de oro sobre la mesa. Los ojos del gigante comenzaron a dolerle al mirar el brillo del oro. Así que los cerró.

Jack and the Beanstalk

Jack and the Beanstalk

Jack and the Beanstalk

As soon as the giant fell asleep, Jack grabbed the goose. Then, he quickly slid down the beanstalk.

Tan pronto como el gigante se durmió, Juan agarró al ganso. Luego, se deslizó rápidamente por el tallo de frijoles.

Jack and the Beanstalk

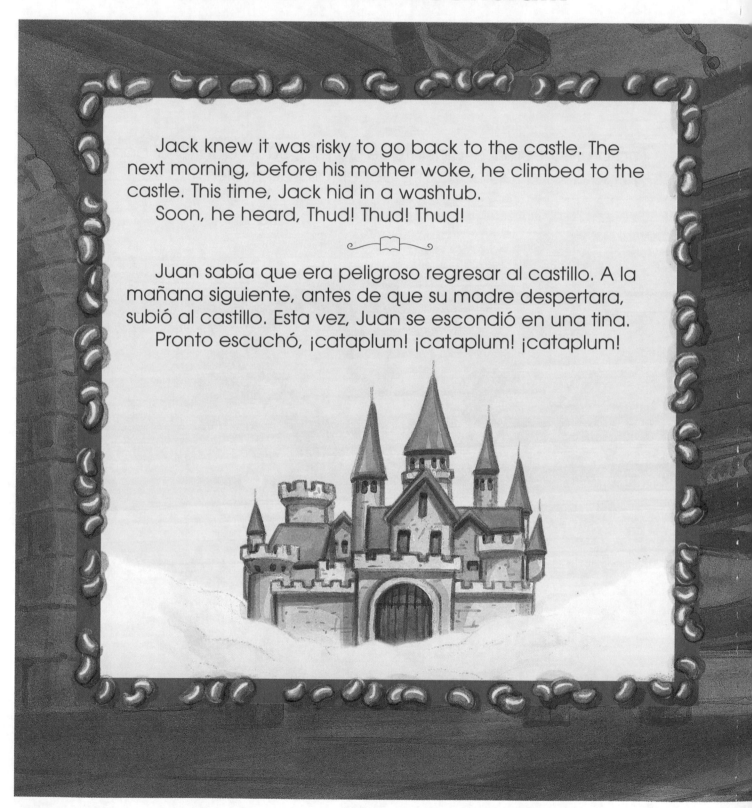

Jack knew it was risky to go back to the castle. The next morning, before his mother woke, he climbed to the castle. This time, Jack hid in a washtub.

Soon, he heard, Thud! Thud! Thud!

Juan sabía que era peligroso regresar al castillo. A la mañana siguiente, antes de que su madre despertara, subió al castillo. Esta vez, Juan se escondió en una tina.

Pronto escuchó, ¡cataplum! ¡cataplum! ¡cataplum!

Jack and the Beanstalk

Jack and the Beanstalk

Jack and the Beanstalk

The giant came in. He took one sniff and said, "Fee, fi, foe, fum! I smell—"

"You certainly do," interrupted his wife. "That little thief is probably hiding in the cupboard."

But Jack was not there.

After breakfast, the giant got out a golden harp.

"Play!" he roared.

El gigante entró, husmeó una vez y dijo—: ¡Ummm! ¡Ñam! ¡Ñam! ¡Huelo…

—Sin duda, —interrumpió su esposa—. Ese pequeño ladrón probablemente esté escondido en el armario.

Pero Juan no estaba ahí.

Después del desayuno, el gigante sacó un arpa de oro.

—¡Toca! —rugió.

Jack and the Beanstalk

The beautiful harp music put the giant to sleep. Jack grabbed the harp, and it screamed, "Master! Master!" The giant woke and ran after Jack.

La hermosa música del arpa hizo dormir al gigante. Juan agarró el arpa y esta gritó—: ¡Maestro! ¡Maestro! El gigante se despertó y salió corriendo detrás de Juan.

Jack and the Beanstalk

Nombre_____

Jack and the Beanstalk

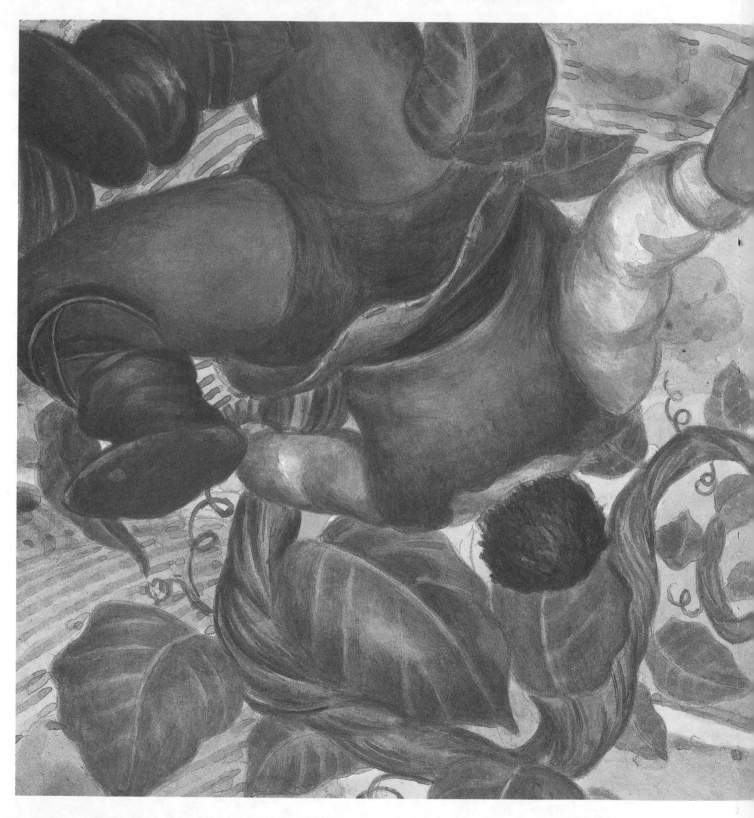

Nombre_____

Jack and the Beanstalk

Jack scrambled down the beanstalk to his mother.
He grabbed an ax and whacked at the stalk until it snapped in two. The giant and the beanstalk crashed to the ground.
And that was the end of the giant.

Juan bajó con dificultad por el tallo de frijoles hasta donde estaba su madre.
Agarró un hacha y golpeó el tallo hasta que se rompió en dos. El gigante y el tallo de frijoles se estrellaron contra el suelo.
Y ese fue el final del gigante.

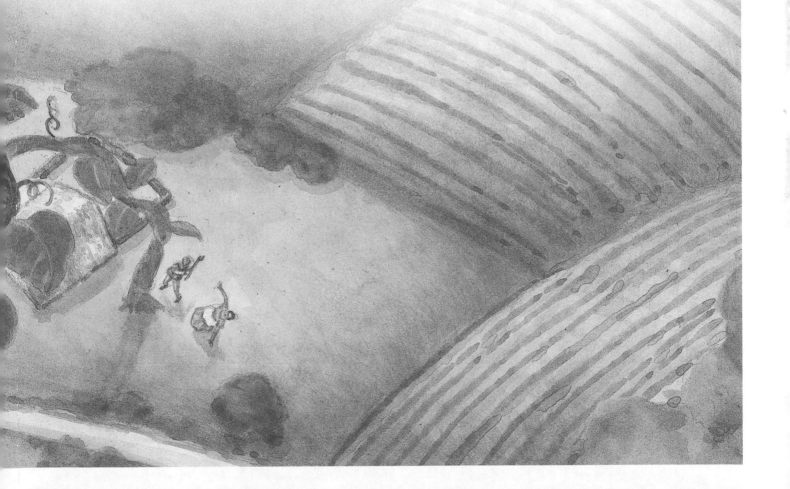

Jack and the Beanstalk

Jack, his mother, the goose, and the harp lived happily ever after.

Juan, su mamá, el ganso y el arpa vivieron felices para siempre.

Nombre_____

Learning Cards

In this section, students will be able to review the topics they have learned earlier in this book. Beginning on page 279, students will be able to cut out and create illustrated books with the vocabulary words from *The Complete Book of Spanish*.

Beginning on page 325, students can cut out flash cards with a Spanish word on one side and the definition in English on the other side. These flash cards are ideal for both individual and group practice.

Learning Cards Table of Contents

This page has been
intentionally left blank.

Introductions and Greetings

¡Hola!

¿Cómo te llamas?

Me llamo

¡Adiós!

¿Cómo estás?

bien

This page has been
intentionally left blank.

Nombre_____

Introductions and Greetings

mal

así, así

¿Cuántos años tienes?

Tengo _____ años.

sí

no

This page has been
intentionally left blank.

Nombre_____

Introductions and Greetings

por favor	gracias
amigo	amiga
amigos	¡Hasta luego!

This page has been
intentionally left blank.

Numbers

0 cero	1 uno 
2 dos 	3 tres 
4 cuatro 	5 cinco 

This page has been
intentionally left blank.

Numbers and the Face (cara)

6 seis

7 siete

8 ocho

9 nueve

10 diez

cara

This page has been
intentionally left blank.

Nombre_____

Numbers

11 once

12 doce

13 trece

14 catorce

15 quince

16 dieciséis

This page has been
intentionally left blank.

Nombre_____

Numbers and Family

17 diecisiete

18 dieciocho

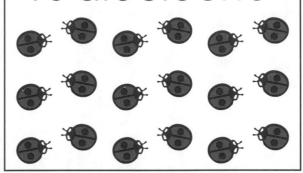

19 diecinueve

20 veinte

hermano

hermana

This page has been
intentionally left blank.

Family

padre

madre

hermano

hermana

abuelo

abuela

This page has been
intentionally left blank.

Nombre_____

The Face

ojos

boca

nariz

dientes

orejas

pelo

This page has been
intentionally left blank.

Nombre_____

Colors

rojo

azul

verde

anaranjado

morado

amarillo

This page has been
intentionally left blank.

Colors and Food

marrón

negro

blanco

rosado

pollo

queso

This page has been
intentionally left blank.

Nombre_____

Food

ensalada

pan

jugo

leche

papa

naranja

This page has been
intentionally left blank.

Food

carne

plátano

sopa

agua

sándwich

manzana

This page has been
intentionally left blank.

Classroom Objects

silla

mesa

tijeras

libro

lápiz

borrador

This page has been
intentionally left blank.

Classroom Objects

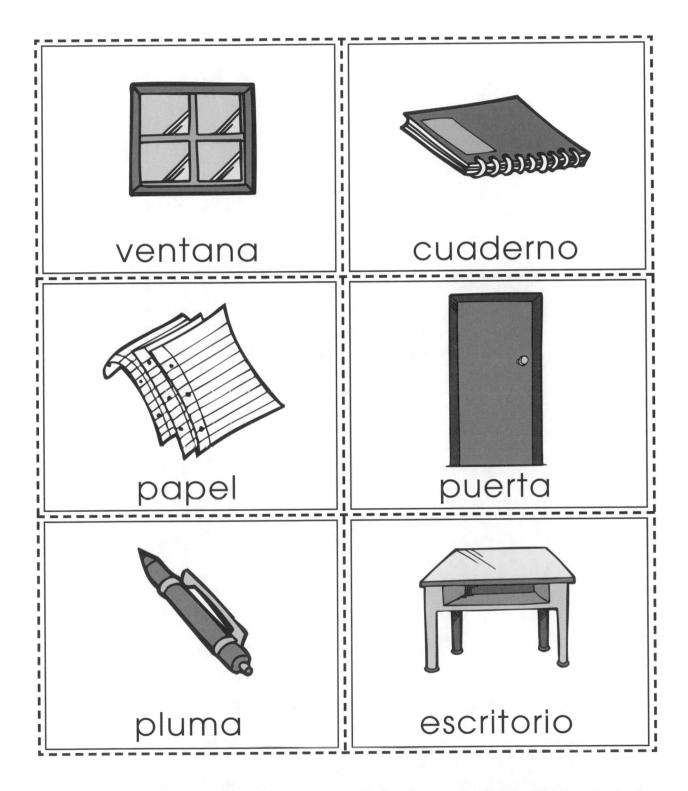

ventana

cuaderno

papel

puerta

pluma

escritorio

This page has been
intentionally left blank.

Clothing

camisa

pantalones

vestido

calcetines

zapatos

gorra

Clothing

chaqueta

pantalones cortos

botas

guantes

falda

abrigo

This page has been
intentionally left blank.

Animals

gato

perro

pájaro

pez

pato

culebra

This page has been
intentionally left blank.

Community

escuela

tienda

museo

biblioteca

casa

parque

This page has been
intentionally left blank.

Nombre_____

Cover Directions

Cut out the ten covers, one cover per unit.

Me llamo

_____

My

Book

Me llamo

_____

My

Book

This page has been intentionally left blank.

Nombre_____

Me llamo

_____

My

Book

Me llamo

_____

My

Book

This page has been
intentionally left blank.

Nombre___________________________

Me llamo

____

My

Book

Me llamo

____

My

Book

Me llamo

____

My

Book

This page has been
intentionally left blank.

Nombre_____

Me llamo

_____

My

Book

Me llamo

_____

My

Book

Me llamo

_____

My

Book

This page has been
intentionally left blank.

Numbers

uno	**cuatro**
dos	**cinco**
tres	**seis**

Numbers

four	one
five	two
six	three

Nombre_____

Numbers

siete

diez

ocho

once

nueve

doce

Numbers

ten	**seven**
eleven	**eight**
twelve	**nine**

Numbers

trece	**dieciséis**
catorce	**diecisiete**
quince	**dieciocho**

Numbers

sixteen	**thirteen**
seventeen	**fourteen**
eighteen	**fifteen**

Nombre_____

Numbers

diecinueve	**veintidós**
veinte	**veintitrés**
veintiuno	**veinticuatro**

Numbers

twenty-two	**nineteen**
twenty-three	**twenty**
twenty-four	**twenty-one**

Numbers/Expressions

veinticinco

las doce

Vamos a contar.

la una

¿Qué hora es?

las dos

Time/Expressions

twelve o'clock	**twenty-five**
one o'clock	**Let's count.**
two o'clock	**What time is it?**

Time

las tres	**las seis**
las cuatro	**las siete**
las cinco	**las ocho**

Time

six o'clock	three o'clock
seven o'clock	four o'clock
eight o'clock	five o'clock

Nombre_____

Time

las nueve	hora
las diez	minuto
las once	segundo

Time

hour	**nine o'clock**
minute	**ten o'clock**
second	**eleven o'clock**

Verbs

levántense	**cierren**
siéntense	**cállense**
abran	**pónganse en fila**

Verbs

close	**stand up**
be quiet	**sit down**
line up	**open**

Nombre_____

Verbs

paren	**pinten**
corten	**dibujen**
peguen	**canten**

Nombre_____

Verbs

paint	**stop**
draw	**cut**
sing	**paste**

Verbs

saquen	**contar**
mirar	**escribir**
escuchar	**leer**

Verbs

to count	take out
to write	to look
to read	to listen

Verbs

comer	**limpiar**
hablar	**dormir**
beber	**tocar**

Verbs

to clean	**to eat**
to sleep	**to speak**
to touch	**to drink**

Nombre_____

Expressions

dar	**por favor**
hola	**gracias**
adiós	**vengan aquí**

Expressions

please	to give
thank you	hello
come here	good-bye

Expressions

anden por favor	¿Cómo te llamas?
sí	¿Cómo estás?
¿Hablas español?	¿Qué día es hoy?

Nombre_____

Expressions

What is
your name?

please walk.

How are you?

yes

What day
is today?

Do you speak
Spanish?

Expressions

Estoy bien.	**¡Buenos días!**
Hoy es lunes.	**¡Buenas tardes!**
¡Mucho gusto!	**¡Buenas noches!**

Expressions

Good morning!

I am fine.

Good afternoon!

Today is Monday.

Good night!

Pleased to meet you!

Nombre_____

Expressions and Days of the Week

¡Hasta luego!	**miércoles**
lunes	**jueves**
martes	**viernes**

Expressions and Days of the Week

Wednesday	**See you later!**
Thursday	**Monday**
Friday	**Tuesday**

Days of the Week and Months

sábado	**febrero**
domingo	**marzo**
enero	**abril**

 Nombre_______________

Days of the Week and Months

February	Saturday
March	Sunday
April	January

Nombre_____

Months

mayo	**agosto**
junio	**septiembre**
julio	**octubre**

Months

August	**May**
September	**June**
October	**July**

Nombre_____

Months and Colors

noviembre

verde

diciembre

anaranjado

rojo

amarillo

Nombre ____________________

Months and Colors

green	November
orange	December
yellow	red

Nombre_____

Colors

azul

blanco

morado

rosado

negro

marrón

Colors

white

blue

pink

purple

brown

black

Clothing

la camisa	el suéter
los pantalones	la chaqueta
el vestido	los zapatos

Clothing

sweater

shirt

jacket

pants

shoes

dress

Clothing

los calcetines	**la falda**
la gorra	**los guantes**
las botas	**el cinturón**

Clothing

skirt

socks

gloves

cap

belt

boots

School

la escuela	la clase
el maestro	los estudiantes
la maestra	el libro

School

classroom	**school**
students	**teacher** (male)
book	**teacher** (female)

School

el lápiz	**el cuaderno**
el papel	**las tijeras**
el borrador	**la pluma**

School

notebook	**pencil**
scissors	**paper**
pen	**eraser**

School

salida

el escritorio

el reloj

la mochila

la silla

la regla

School

desk	**exit**
backpack	**clock**
ruler	**chair**

School

el crayón	**la escritura**
la lectura	**el inglés**
las matemáticas	**las ciencias**

Nombre_____

School

handwriting	crayon
English	reading
science	math

School/Shapes

estudios sociales

el rectangulo

el circulo

el triángulo

el cuardrado

el diamante

School/Shapes

rectangle

social studies

triangle

circle

diamond

square

Final Review

tú

lean

tres

¡Hola!

 madre

 queso

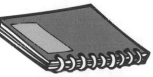 cuaderno

rosado

camisa

ojos

escuela

 gato

feo

Final Review

For each English word given, write the Spanish word with the same meaning. Use the number of blanks as clues. Can you find the hidden word spelled down in each list?

four ___ ___ | ___ ___ ___   mother ___ ___ | ___ ___

hand ___ | ___ ___ ___   kitchen ___ ___ | ___ ___ ___

blue ___ | ___ ___ ___   clean ___ ___ | ___ ___ ___

fruit ___ | ___ ___ ___   thirty ___ ___ | ___ ___ ___

chair ___ | ___ ___ ___   paint ___ ___ | ___ ___

church ___ ___ | ___ ___ ___ ___   friend (m) ___ ___ ___ | ___

hello ___ ___ | ___ ___   to eat ___ | ___ ___ ___

boots ___ | ___ ___ ___

the letter h ___ ___ | ___ ___   Hidden Words

Saturday ___ ___ ___ | ___ ___   1._____

horse ___ ___ ___ | ___ ___   2._____

milk ___ ___ | ___ ___   3._____

black ___ ___ | ___ ___

you (formal) ___ ___ | ___ ___

goodbye ___ ___ | ___ ___

store ___ ___ | ___ ___

teacher (female) ___ ___ | ___ ___ ___

hat ___ | ___ ___ ___ ___ ___

Handwriting Practice

After each lesson, use handwriting practice to reinforce the new vocabulary. The vocabulary is organized by lesson. Write the Spanish words from the recent (or past) lesson on the lines provided on pages 381 and 382.

Vocabulary Organized by Lesson

Numbers
cero
uno
dos
tres
cuatro
cinco
seis
siete
ocho
nueve
diez
once
doce
trece
catorce
quince
dieciséis
diecisiete
dieciocho
diecinueve
veinte
veintiuno
veintidós
veintitrés
veinticuatro
veinticinco
veintiséis
veintisiete
veintiocho
veintinueve
treinta

Colors
rojo
azul
verde
anaranjado
morado
amarillo
marrón
negro
blanco
rosado

Basic Expressions
Me llamo
¿Cómo estás?
Estoy bien.
Estoy mal.
Estoy así así.
¿Cuántos años tienes?
Tengo ____ años.
hola
amigo
amiga

sí
no
por favor
gracias
¡Hasta luego!
adiós
maestro
maestra
señor
señora
señorita
¡Buenos días!
¡Buenas tardes!
¡Buenas noches!
Vamos a contar.

Days of the Week
lunes
martes
miércoles
jueves
viernes
sábado
domingo
hoy
ayer
mañana

Classroom Objects
silla
mesa
tijeras
libro
lápiz
borrador
ventana
puerta
papel
cuaderno
escritorio
pluma

Clothing
falda
cinturón
chaqueta
calcetines
camisa
vestido
sombrero
pantalones
guantes
botas
zapatos
pantalones cortos

Handwriting Practice

Food
ensalada
plátano
manzana
papa
pan
naranja
queso
carne
sopa
fruta
jugo
vegetales
sándwich
leche
agua
pollo

Community
escuela
iglesia
casa
biblioteca
tienda
parque
museo
apartamento
cine
granja
restaurante
zoológico

The Body
cuerpo
cabeza
mano
pierna
hombro
brazo
dedo
pie
rodilla
estómago
cara
ojos
orejas
pelo
boca
nariz
dientes

The Family
hermano
hija
hermana
padre
tío
primos
abuelo
familia
abuela
hijo
madre
tía

Animals
gato
perro
pájaro
pez
pato
oso
rana
caballo
vaca
abeja

The House
casa
cocina
sala
dormitorio
cama
cuchara
lámpara
sofá

Adjectives
feliz
nuevo
pequeño
feo
limpio
sucio
bonita
triste
viejo
grande

Commands
corten
peguen
pinten
canten
abran
cierren
levántense
siéntense
párense
dibujen

Verbs
comer
beber
dormir
tocar
hablar
limpiar
mirar
dar

Handwriting Practice

Nombre_____

Handwriting Practice

Nombre_____

Glossary

abeja	bee	catorce	fourteen
abran	open	cero	zero
abrigo	coat	chaqueta	jacket
abuela	grandmother	cierren	close
abuelo	grandfather	cinco	five
adiós	goodbye	cine	movie theater
agua	water	cinturón	belt
amarillo	yellow	ciudad	city
amiga	friend (f)	cocina	kitchen
amigo	friend (m)	comer	to eat
anaranjado	orange	contar	to count
años	years	corten	cut
apartamento	apartment	cuaderno	notebook
así así	so-so	cuatro	four
ayer	yesterday	cuchara	spoon
azul	blue	cuerpo	body
beber	drink	dar	to give
biblioteca	library	dedo	finger/toe
bien	well/fine	día	day
blanco	white	dibujen	draw
blusa	blouse	diecinueve	nineteen
boca	mouth	dieciocho	twenty-eight
bonito	pretty	dieciséis	sixteen
borrador	eraser	diecisiete	seventeen
botas	boots	dientes	teeth
brazo	arm	diez	ten
caballo	horse	doce	twelve
cabeza	head	domingo	Sunday
café	brown	dormir	to sleep
calcetines	socks	dormitorio	bedroom
cama	bed	dos	two
camisa	shirt	ensalada	salad
canten	sing	escritorio	desk
cara	face	escuela	school
carne	meat	estoy	I am
casa	house	estómago	stomach

Glossary

falda	skirt		*martes*	Tuesday
familia	family		*Me llamo*	My name is
feliz	happy		*mesa*	table
feo	ugly		*miércoles*	Wednesday
fruta	fruit		*mirar*	to look at
gato	cat		*morado*	purple
gracias	thank you		*museo*	museum
grande	big		*naranja*	orange
granja	farm		*nariz*	nose
guantes	gloves		*negro*	black
hablar	to speak		*no*	no
hermana	sister		*noches*	night
hermano	brother		*nueve*	nine
hija	daughter		*nuevo*	new
hijo	son		*ocho*	eight
hola	hello		*ojos*	eyes
hombro	shoulder		*once*	eleven
hoy	today		*orejas*	ears
iglesia	church		*oso*	bear
jueves	Thursday		*padre*	father
jugo	juice		*pájaro*	bird
lámpara	lamp		*pan*	bread
lápiz	pencil		*pantalones*	pants
leche	milk		*pantalones cortos*	shorts
levántense	stand up		*papa*	potato
libro	book		*papel*	paper
limpiar	to clean		*parque*	park
limpio	clean		*pato*	duck
lunes	Monday		*paren*	stop
madre	mother		*peguen*	glue
maestra	teacher (f)		*pelo*	hair
maestro	teacher (m)		*pequeño*	small
mal	bad, not well		*perro*	dog
mano	hand		*pez*	fish
manzana	apple		*pie*	foot
mañana	tomorrow		*pierna*	leg

Glossary

pinten	paint	tío	uncle
plátano	banana	tocar	to touch
pluma	pen	trece	thirteen
pollo	chicken	treinta	thirty
por favor	please	tres	three
primos	cousins	triste	sad
puerta	door	uno	one
queso	cheese	vaca	cow
quince	fifteen	Vamos a contar.	Let's count.
rana	frog	vegetales	vegetables
restaurante	restaurant	veinte	twenty
rodilla	knee	veinticinco	twenty-five
rojo	red	veinticuatro	twenty-four
rosado	pink	veintidós	twenty-two
sala	room	veintinueve	twenty-nine
sandalias	sandals	veintiocho	twenty-eight
sándwich	sandwich	veintiséis	twenty-six
sábado	Saturday	veintisiete	twenty-seven
seis	six	veintitrés	twenty-three
señor	Mr.	veintiuno	twenty-one
señora	Mrs.	ventana	window
señorita	Miss	verde	green
siete	seven	vestido	dress
siéntense	sit down	viejo	old
silla	chair	viernes	Friday
sí	yes	zapatos	shoes
sofá	couch	zoológico	zoo
sombrero	hat	¿Cómo estás?	How are you? (familiar)
sopa	soup	¿Cuántos años tienes?	How old are you? (familiar)
sucio	dirty		
tardes	afternoon	¡Buenas noches!	Good night!
Tengo ___ años.	I am __ years old.	¡Buenas tardes!	Good afternoon!
tienda	store	¡Buenos días!	Good morning!
tienes	you are	¡Hasta luego!	See you later!
tijeras	scissors		
tía	aunt		

Literature

Your child will enjoy listening to stories in Spanish. There are many excellent and familiar children's books available in Spanish. The books have beautiful art that engages your child and assists in comprehension. The bibliography is organized to help you choose the books related to the topics taught in *The Complete Book of Spanish*. Whenever possible, read the book first in Spanish and then in English.

Reading out loud to your child in Spanish will stretch them intellectually. Although much of the vocabulary may be unfamiliar, your child will be able to follow the basic story line in Spanish. Your child will gain exposure to the language as they listen to a familiar story, look at the pictures, and strain to catch words they may know.

Before you read, discuss the story. Turn the pages and ask your child to predict what the story might be about. Encourage your child to name pictured items in Spanish. Activate prior knowledge by discussing your child's experiences with the book's topic. When your child is engaged, begin reading.

As you read in Spanish, stop periodically to check for understanding. Ask brief questions about the actions of the characters. Acknowledge your child's predictions as they occur in the story. Quickly explain things that you think your child might have missed. Keep the rhythm of the story as much as you can. Keep your comprehension checks brief so you do not lose your child's attention.

After reading, discuss the story and conduct activities related to the book topic. Ask questions that require your child to think back to the story line or reread passages. Ask your child to explain why an event happened in the story. Review vocabulary that is familiar to your child. Read the book out loud several times. Allow your child to choose the book during independent reading time.

As you reread a book, ask your child to read out loud with you. This works especially well in stories that have repetition or predictable passages. Practice the lines in Spanish that you want your child to read out loud.

Most importantly, have fun with your child. Celebrate the joy of reading in a new language. Listen to the beauty of the language and enjoy the pictures.

Nombre_____

Bibliography of Children's Literature

Name of Book	Author	Language	Related Topics
A la cama	Moira Kemp Mathew Price	Spanish	animals
Azulín visita a México	Virginia Poulet	Spanish	Mexico
Buenas noches, luna Goodnight, Moon	Margaret Wise Brown	Spanish English	house, general
¿Cuántos son?	Maribel Suárez	Spanish	numbers
Cuenta con Gato Galano	Donald Charles	Spanish	numbers
El Conejo Andarín The Runaway Bunny	Margaret Wise Brown	Spanish English	animals, family, general
El tesoro de Azulín	Virginia Poulet	Spanish	adjectives
Gordito, Gordón, Gato Galano	Donald Charles	Spanish	food
Huevos verdes con jamón Green Eggs and Ham	Dr. Seuss	Spanish English	food, general
Los gatitos The Kitten Book	Jan Pflogg	Spanish English	animals
¿Has visto a mi patito?	Nancy Tafuri	Spanish	animals

Bibliography of Children's Literature

Name of Book	Author	Language	Related Topics
La primera Navidad de Clifford Clifford's First Christmas	Norman Bridwell	Spanish English	Christmas
La ropa	Moira Kemp Mathew Price	Spanish	clothes, animals
La semilla de zanahoria	Ruth Krauss	Spanish	food (carrot), general vocabulary
Let's Eat	Hideo Shirotani	bilingual	food
Los colores	Maribel Suárez	Spanish	colors
Mi primera visita al zoo	J. M. Parramón G. Sales	Spanish	animals
Mis primeros colores	Isidro Sánchez	Spanish	colors
Mis primeros números	Isidro Sánchez	Spanish	numbers
Osos, osos, aquí y allí	Rita Milios	Spanish	animals (bears)
Perro grande, perro pequeño Big Dog, Little Dog	P. D. Eastman	bilingual	adjectives, general vocabulary
¿Qué color? What Color?	Hideo Shirotani	bilingual	colors

Nombre_____

Bibliography of Children's Literature

Name of Book	Author	Language	Related Topics
¿Quién es la bestia?	Keith Baker	Spanish	animals
Salí de paseo	Sue Williams	Spanish	animals
Say Hola to Spanish	Susan Middleton Elya	bilingual	introduction to the language
Se venden gorras Hats for Sale	Esphyr Slobodkina	Spanish English	clothing, animals, general
Somos un arco iris	Nancy María Grande Tabor	bilingual	cultural awareness
Esta casa está hecha de lodo This House Is Made of Mud	Ken Buchanan	bilingual	house, general
Too Many Tamales	Gary Soto	English	cultural awareness
Un día feliz	Ruth Krauss	Spanish	animals
Un murmullo es silencioso	Carolyn Lunn	Spanish	adjectives, general vocabulary
Yo soy	Rita Milios	Spanish	self-adjectives, general vocabulary

Answer Key

Page 8

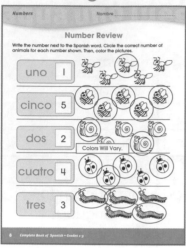

Page 9

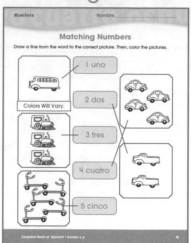

Page 10

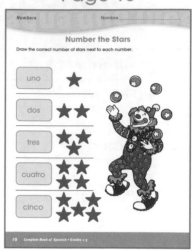

Page 11

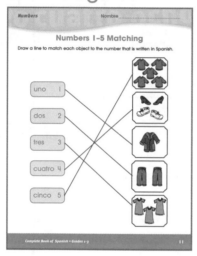

Page 12

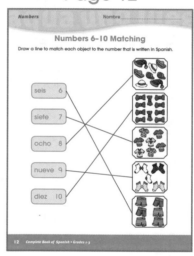

Page 13

Page 14

Page 15

Page 16

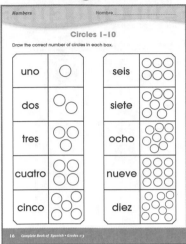

Circles 1-10

Draw the correct number of circles in each box.

uno	○	seis	○○○
dos	○○	siete	○○○
tres	○○○	ocho	○○○
cuatro	○○○○	nueve	○○○
cinco	○○○○○	diez	○○○

Page 17

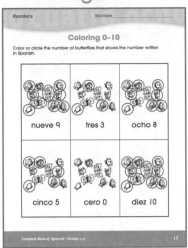

Coloring 0-10

Color or circle the number of butterflies that shows the number written in Spanish.

nueve 9	tres 3	ocho 8
cinco 5	cero 0	diez 10

Page 18

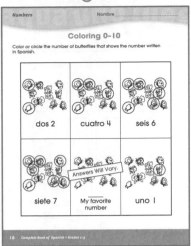

Coloring 0-10

Color or circle the number of butterflies that shows the number written in Spanish.

dos 2	cuatro 4	seis 6
siete 7	My favorite number (Answers Will Vary)	uno 1

Page 19

Numbers 0-10

Trace and write each of the number words from 0 to 10 in Spanish. Use the words at the left to help you.

```
0  cero    cero    cero  cero  cero
1  uno     uno     uno   uno   uno
2  dos     dos     dos   dos   dos
3  tres    tres    tres  tres  tres
4  cuatro  cuatro  cuatro  cuatro
5  cinco   cinco   cinco  cinco
6  seis    seis    seis  seis  seis
7  siete   siete   siete  siete
8  ocho    ocho    ocho  ocho  ocho
9  nueve   nueve   nueve  nueve
10 diez    diez    diez  diez  diez
```

Page 20

Numbers 0-10

Say each word out loud. Circle the number that tells the meaning of the word.

seis	5	0	⑥
ocho	1	9	⑧
uno	3	①	8
cero	8	10	⓪
siete	9	⑦	1
tres	0	③	5
diez	⑩	8	7
nueve	4	2	⑨
cuatro	7	5	④
dos	②	6	3
cinco	6	4	⑤

Page 21

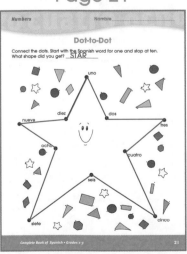

Dot-to-Dot

Connect the dots. Start with the Spanish word for one and stop at ten. What shape did you get? __STAR__

Page 22

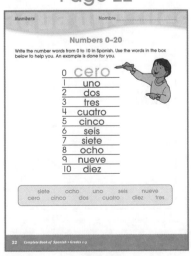

Numbers 0-20

Write the number words from 0 to 10 in Spanish. Use the words in the box below to help you. An example is done for you.

```
0  cero
1  uno
2  dos
3  tres
4  cuatro
5  cinco
6  seis
7  siete
8  ocho
9  nueve
10 diez
```

siete	ocho	uno	seis	nueve
cero	cinco	dos	cuatro	diez	tres

Page 23

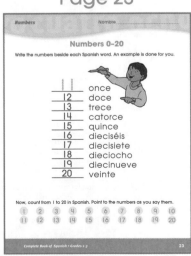

Numbers 0-20

Write the numbers beside each Spanish word. An example is done for you.

11	once
12	doce
13	trece
14	catorce
15	quince
16	dieciséis
17	diecisiete
18	dieciocho
19	diecinueve
20	veinte

Now, count from 1 to 20 in Spanish. Point to the numbers as you say them.

1 2 3 4 5 6 7 8 9 10
11 12 13 14 15 16 17 18 19 20

Answer Key

Page 24

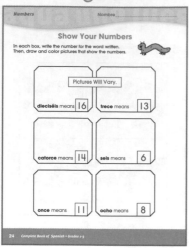

Numbers Nombre_____

Show Your Numbers

In each box, write the number for the word written.
Then, draw and color pictures that show the numbers.

Pictures Will Vary.

dieciséis means 16 **trece** means 13

catorce means 14 **seis** means 6

once means 11 **ocho** means 8

24 *Complete Book of Spanish • Grades 1-3*

Page 25

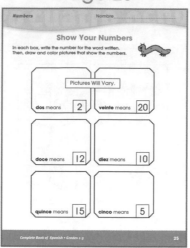

Numbers Nombre_____

Show Your Numbers

In each box, write the number for the word written.
Then, draw and color pictures that show the numbers.

Pictures Will Vary.

dos means 2 **veinte** means 20

doce means 12 **diez** means 10

quince means 15 **cinco** means 5

Complete Book of Spanish • Grades 1-3 25

Page 26

Numbers Nombre_____

Sunshine 0–20

Write the number for each Spanish word. Cross out the correct number of
suns to show the number written in Spanish. The first one is done for you.

quince 15 veinte 20

once 11 nueve 9

tres 3 trece 13

26 *Complete Book of Spanish • Grades 1-3*

Page 27

Numbers Nombre_____

Sunshine 0–20

Write the number for each Spanish word. Cross out the correct number of
suns to show the number written in Spanish.

catorce 14 dieciocho 18

doce 12 My favorite number

Anwers will vary.

cero 0 seis 6

Complete Book of Spanish • Grades 1-3 27

Page 28

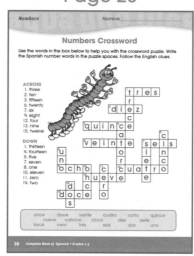

Numbers Nombre_____

Numbers Crossword

Use the words in the box below to help you with the crossword puzzle. Write
the Spanish number words in the puzzle spaces. Follow the English clues.

ACROSS
1. three
2. ten
3. fifteen
6. twenty
7. six
9. eight
12. four
13. nine
15. twelve

DOWN
1. thirteen
4. fourteen
5. five
7. seven
8. one
10. eleven
11. zero
14. two

once doce veinte cuatro ocho quince
nueve catorce cinco diez siete
trece cero tres seis dos uno

28 *Complete Book of Spanish • Grades 1-3*

Page 29

Numbers Nombre_____

Numbers

After each numeral, write the number word in Spanish. Refer to the words
below to help you.

Word Bank

veinte cuatro trece siete cinco
doce once cero ocho seis
catorce dos dieciocho diecisiete quince
diecinueve nueve diez uno tres
 dieciséis

0 cero 11 once
1 uno 12 doce
2 dos 13 trece
3 tres 14 catorce
4 cuatro 15 quince
5 cinco 16 dieciséis
6 seis 17 diecisiete
7 siete 18 dieciocho
8 ocho 19 diecinueve
9 nueve 20 veinte
10 diez

Complete Book of Spanish • Grades 1-3 29

Page 30

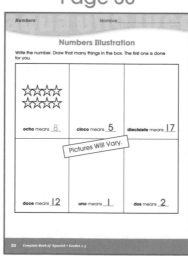

Numbers Nombre_____

Numbers Illustration

Write the number. Draw that many things in the box. The first one is done
for you.

ocho means 8 **cinco** means 5 **diecisiete** means 17

Pictures Will Vary.

doce means 12 **uno** means 1 **dos** means 2

30 *Complete Book of Spanish • Grades 1-3*

Page 31

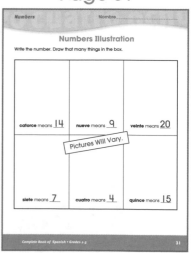

Numbers Nombre_____

Numbers Illustration

Write the number. Draw that many things in the box.

catorce means 14 **nueve** means 9 **veinte** means 20

Pictures Will Vary.

siete means 7 **cuatro** means 4 **quince** means 15

Complete Book of Spanish • Grades 1-3 31

Page 32

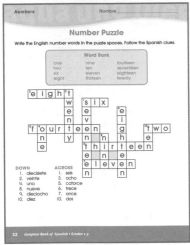

Numbers   Nombre_____

Number Puzzle

Write the English number words in the puzzle spaces. Follow the Spanish clues.

Word Bank

one	nine	fourteen
two	ten	seventeen
six	eleven	eighteen
eight	thirteen	twenty

Crossword solution:
- ¹e i g h t
- ⁴t w e n t y
- ⁵s i x
- ⁶e i g h t
- ⁷f o u r t e e n
- t w o
- o n e
- ⁸t h i r t e e n
- e l e v e n

DOWN
1. diecisiete
2. veinte
4. uno
8. nueve
9. dieciocho
10. diez

ACROSS
1. seis
3. ocho
5. catorce
6. trece
7. once
10. dos

Page 33

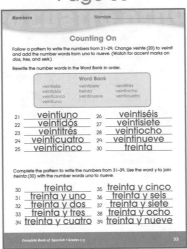

Numbers   Nombre_____

Counting On

Follow a pattern to write the numbers from 21–29. Change *veinte* (20) to *veinti* and add the number words from *uno* to *nueve*. (Watch for accent marks on *dos, tres,* and *seis*.)

Rewrite the number words in the Word Bank in order.

Word Bank

veintiséis	veintisiete	veintitrés
veintidós	treinta	veintiocho
veinticinco	veintinueve	veinticuatro
veintiuno		

21	veintiuno	26	veintiséis
22	veintidós	27	veintisiete
23	veintitrés	28	veintiocho
24	veinticuatro	29	veintinueve
25	veinticinco	30	treinta

Complete the pattern to write the numbers from 31–39. Use the word *y* to join *treinta* (30) with the number words *uno* to *nueve*.

30	treinta	35	treinta y cinco
31	treinta y uno	36	treinta y seis
32	treinta y dos	37	treinta y siete
33	treinta y tres	38	treinta y ocho
34	treinta y cuatro	39	treinta y nueve

Page 34

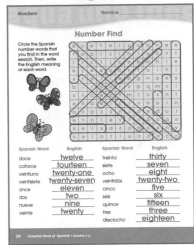

Numbers   Nombre_____

Number Find

Circle the Spanish number words that you find in the word search. Then, write the English meaning of each word.

Spanish Word	English	Spanish Word	English
doce	twelve	treinta	thirty
catorce	fourteen	siete	seven
veintiuno	twenty-one	ocho	eight
veintisiete	twenty-seven	veintidós	twenty-two
once	eleven	cinco	five
dos	two	seis	six
nueve	nine	quince	fifteen
veinte	twenty	tres	three
		dieciocho	eighteen

Page 35

Numbers   Nombre_____

Counting by Tens

The Spanish numbers ten, twenty, thirty, forty, and fifty are written out of order below. Write the value of each number word in the blank.

30	treinta	50	cincuenta	40	cuarenta
10	diez	20	veinte		

Write the numbers from 30–59 in Spanish.

30	treinta	45	cuarenta y cinco
31	treinta y uno	46	cuarenta y seis
32	treinta y dos	47	cuarenta y siete
33	treinta y tres	48	cuarenta y ocho
34	treinta y cuatro	49	cuarenta y nueve
35	treinta y cinco	50	cincuenta
36	treinta y seis	51	cincuenta y uno
37	treinta y siete	52	cincuenta y dos
38	treinta y ocho	53	cincuenta y tres
39	treinta y nueve	54	cincuenta y cuatro
40	cuarenta	55	cincuenta y cinco
41	cuarenta y uno	56	cincuenta y seis
42	cuarenta y dos	57	cincuenta y siete
43	cuarenta y tres	58	cincuenta y ocho
44	cuarenta y cuatro	59	cincuenta y nueve

Page 36

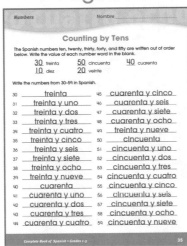

Numbers   Nombre_____

Number Search

Circle the Spanish number words that you find in the word search. Write the English meanings at the bottom of the page next to the Spanish words from the puzzle.

Spanish Word	English	Spanish Word	English
cero	zero	dos	two
cuatro	four	seis	six
ocho	eight	diez	ten
doce	twelve	catorce	fourteen
veinte	twenty	cuarenta	forty
uno	one	tres	three
cinco	five	siete	seven
nueve	nine	once	eleven
trece	thirteen	quince	fifteen
treinta	thirty	cincuenta	fifty

Page 38

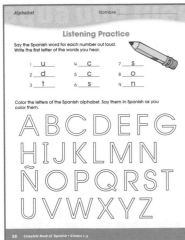

Alphabet   Nombre_____

Listening Practice

Say the Spanish word for each number out loud. Write the first letter of the words you hear.

1. u   4. c   7. s
2. d   5. c   8. o
3. t   6. s   9. n

Color the letters of the Spanish alphabet. Say them in Spanish as you color them.

A B C D E F G
H I J K L M N
Ñ O P Q R S T
U V W X Y Z

Page 39

Alphabet   Nombre_____

The Alphabet

El abecedario (the alphabet)

a a	g ge	m eme	s ese		
b be	h hache	n ene	t te		
c ce	i i	ñ eñe	u u		
ch che	j jota	o o	v ve		
d de	k ka	p pe	w doble u		
e e	l ele	q cu	x equis		
f efe	ll elle	r ere	y i griega		
			z zeta		

Listening Practice

Write each letter of the alphabet as you say it out loud.

1. a   7. f   13. l   19. p   25. v
2. b   8. g   14. ll   20. q   26. w
3. c   9. h   15. m   21. r   27. x
4. ch   10. i   16. n   22. s   28. y
5. d   11. j   17. ñ   23. t   29. z
6. e   12. k   18. o   24. u

Page 40

Alphabet   Nombre_____

The Alphabet

El abecedario (the alphabet)

a a	j jota
b be	k ka
c ce	l ele
ch che	ll elle
d de	m eme
e e	n ene
f efe	ñ eñe
g ge	p pe
h hache	q cu
i i	

r ere   s ese   t te   u u   v ve   w doble u   x equis   y i griega   z zeta

Listening Practice

Write the Spanish word for each number below. Then, spell each word out loud.

1	uno	5	cinco	9	nueve	13	trece
2	dos	6	seis	10	diez	14	catorce
3	tres	7	siete	11	once	15	quince
4	cuatro	8	ocho	12	doce	16	dieciséis

Answer Key

Page 43

Using You

Spanish uses two different forms of the pronoun **you**.

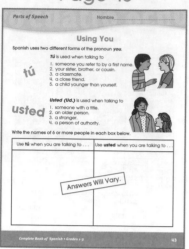

tú is used when talking to
1. someone you refer to by a first name.
2. your sister, brother, or cousin.
3. a classmate.
4. a close friend.
5. a child younger than yourself.

usted

Usted (Ud.) is used when talking to
1. someone with a title.
2. an older person.
3. a stranger.
4. a person of authority.

Write the names of 6 or more people in each box below.

Use **tú** when you are talking to . . .	Use **usted** when you are talking to . . .
Answers Will Vary.	

Complete Book of Spanish • Grades 1-3 — 43

Page 44

Picking Pronouns

Spanish uses two different forms of the pronoun **you**.

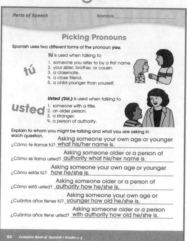

tú is used when talking to
1. someone you refer to by a first name.
2. your sister, brother, or cousin.
3. a classmate.
4. a close friend.
5. a child younger than yourself.

usted

Usted (Ud.) is used when talking to
1. someone with a title.
2. an older person.
3. a stranger.
4. a person of authority.

Explain to whom you might be talking and what you are asking in each question.

¿Cómo te llamas tú? **Asking someone your own age or younger what his/her name is.**

¿Cómo se llama usted? **Asking someone older or a person of authority what his/her name is.**

¿Cómo estás tú? **Asking someone your own age or younger how he/she is.**

¿Cómo está usted? **Asking someone older or a person of authority how he/she is.**

¿Cuántos años tienes tú? **Asking someone your own age or younger how old he/she is.**

¿Cuántos años tiene usted? **Asking someone older or a person with authority how old he/she is.**

44 Complete Book of Spanish • Grades 1-3

Page 45

Who Is It?

Write the names of people you may know that fit each description below.

tú-informal or familiar form of you	
someone you refer to by first name	
your sister or brother (or cousin)	
a classmate	*Answers Will Vary.*
a close friend	
a child younger than yourself	

usted-formal or polite form of you	
someone with a title	
an older person	
a stranger	*Answers Will Vary.*
a person of authority	

How would you speak to each person below? Write tú or usted after each person named.

1. Dr. Hackett **usted**
2. Susana **tú**
3. a four-year-old **tú**
4. your grandfather **usted**
5. the governor **usted**
6. your best friend **tú**
7. your sister **tú**
8. the principal **usted**
9. a classmate **tú**
10. a stranger **usted**

45

Page 46

Masculine and Feminine

All Spanish nouns and adjectives have gender. This means they are either masculine or feminine. Here are two basic rules to help determine the gender of words. There are other rules for gender which you will learn as you study more Spanish.

1. Spanish words ending in -o are usually masculine.
2. Spanish words ending in -a are usually feminine.

Write the words on this page and the next page in the charts to determine their gender. Then, write the English words to the right. Use a Spanish-English dictionary if you need help.

Masculine	
words ending in -o	meaning of the word
amigo	friend (male)
rojo	red
libro	book
cuaderno	notebook
escritorio	desk
anaranjado	orange
museo	museum
blanco	white
negro	black
maestro	teacher (male)
abrigo	coat
vestido	dress
queso	cheese

maestra maestro
amigo amiga
silla falda
rojo abrigo
libro vestido
ventana camisa
puerta chaqueta
cuaderno sopa
escritorio fruta
pluma queso
anaranjado tienda
blanco museo
negro casa

46 Complete Book of Spanish • Grades 1-3

Page 47

Masculine and Feminine

Feminine	
words ending in -a	meaning of the word
maestra	teacher (female)
silla	chair
ventana	window
puerta	door
pluma	pen
amiga	friend (female)
falda	skirt
camisa	shirt
chaqueta	jacket
sopa	soup
fruta	fruit
tienda	store
casa	house

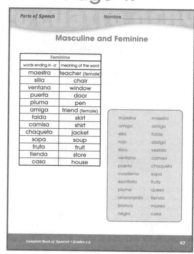

maestra maestro
amigo amiga
silla falda
rojo abrigo
libro vestido
ventana camisa
puerta chaqueta
cuaderno sopa
escritorio fruta
pluma queso
anaranjado tienda
blanco museo
negro casa

47

Page 48

More Than One

Spanish nouns can be placed into two groups—singular nouns (one of something) or plural nouns (more than one of something). Nouns that end in -s are usually plural. Nouns ending in other letters are usually singular.

Read the following familiar nouns. Write **S** if the noun is singular and **P** if the noun is plural.

P 1. calcetines
S 2. dedo
P 3. botas
S 4. cuerpo
P 5. vegetales
S 6. ciudad
S 7. escuela
P 8. sandalias
P 9. zapatos
P 10. guantes
S 11. casa
S 12. boca

Follow these rules to write the following Spanish words in the plural.

1. If the word ends in a vowel, add -s.
2. If the word ends in a consonant, add -es.
3. If the word ends in z, change the z to c before adding -es.

1. carne **carnes**
2. silla **sillas**
3. ciudad **ciudades**
4. lápiz **lápices**
5. azul **azules**
6. nariz **narices**
7. abrigo **abrigos**
8. señor **señores**
9. borrador **borradores**
10. pollo **pollos**

48 Complete Book of Spanish • Grades 1-3

Page 49

More and More

Write the plural form of each Spanish clue word in the puzzle.

Across
1. hombro
4. falda
5. zapato
7. museo
8. nariz
10. gato
11. sombrero
13. oso
14. lápiz

Down
2. borrador
3. vaso
6. escuela
9. casa
12. mesa

Complete Book of Spanish • Grades 1-3 — 49

Page 50

Definite Articles

In Spanish, there are four ways to say "the"—*el, la, los,* and *las.* The definite article (the) agrees with its noun in gender (masculine or feminine) and number (singular or plural).

Masculine singular nouns go with **el**. Feminine singular nouns go with **la**.

Examples: *el libro* (the book)   *el papel* (the paper)
la silla (the chair)   *la regla* (the ruler)

Masculine plural nouns go with **los**. Feminine plural nouns go with **las**.

Examples: *los libros* (the books)   *los papeles* (the papers)
las sillas (the chairs)   *las reglas* (the rulers)

Refer to the Word Bank to complete the chart. Write the singular and plural forms and the correct definite articles. The first ones have been done for you.

Word Bank	cuaderno mesa pluma oso falda
	papel gato bota silla libro

English	Masculine Singular	Masculine Plural
the book	el libro	los libros
the paper	el papel	los papeles
the notebook	el cuaderno	los cuadernos
the cat	el gato	los gatos
the bear	el oso	los osos

English	Feminine Singular	Feminine Plural
the chair	la silla	las sillas
the table	la mesa	las mesas
the boot	la bota	las botas
the skirt	la falda	las faldas
the pen	la pluma	las plumas

50 Complete Book of Spanish • Grades 1-3

Page 51

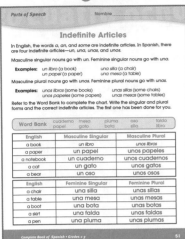

Parts of Speech — Nombre _____

Indefinite Articles

In English, the words *a*, *an*, and *some* are indefinite articles. In Spanish, there are four indefinite articles—*un*, *una*, *unas*, and *unos*.

Masculine singular nouns go with *un*. Feminine singular nouns go with *una*.

Examples: un libro (a book) una silla (a chair)
un papel (a paper) una mesa (a table)

Masculine plural nouns go with *unos*. Feminine plural nouns go with *unas*.

Examples: unos libros (some books) unas sillas (some chairs)
unos papeles (some papers) unas mesas (some tables)

Refer to the Word Bank to complete the chart. Write the singular and plural forms and the correct indefinite articles. The first one has been done for you.

Word Bank: cuaderno mesa pluma oso falda papel gato bota silla libro

English	Masculine Singular	Masculine Plural
a book	un libro	unos libros
a paper	un papel	unos papeles
a notebook	un cuaderno	unos cuadernos
a cat	un gato	unos gatos
a bear	un oso	unos osos

English	Feminine Singular	Feminine Plural
a chair	una silla	unas sillas
a table	una mesa	unas mesas
a boot	una bota	unas botas
a skirt	una falda	unas faldas
a pen	una pluma	unas plumas

Complete Book of Spanish • Grades 1-3   51

Page 52

Parts of Speech — Nombre _____

Articles and Nouns

Refer to the given articles and nouns to translate the following phrases into Spanish. Use a Spanish-English dictionary if you need help.

Articles: un una unos unas el la los las

Nouns: cine (m) cuerpo museo cuadernos cara falda boca caballos blusa elefantes (m) tijeras camas dedo cucharas

1. a skirt — una falda
2. the body — el cuerpo
3. the spoons — las cucharas
4. the mouth — la boca
5. the elephants — los elefantes
6. some scissors — unas tijeras
7. the finger — el dedo
8. a museum — un museo
9. the face — la cara
10. a blouse — una blusa
11. the horses — los caballos
12. some notebooks — unos cuadernos
13. the beds — las camas
14. a movie theater — un cine

52   Complete Book of Spanish • Grades 1-3

Page 53

Parts of Speech — Nombre _____

Pretty Colors

Adjectives are words that tell about or describe nouns. Color each box as indicated in Spanish. Use a Spanish-English dictionary if you need help.

rojo azul verde anaranjado morado
amarillo marrón negro blanco rosado

Here are some new adjectives. Copy the Spanish adjectives in the boxes. Write the Spanish words next to the English words at the bottom of the page.

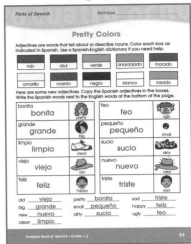

bonita — bonita (pretty)	feo — feo (ugly)
grande — grande (big)	pequeño — pequeño (small)
limpio — limpio (clean)	sucio — sucio (dirty)
viejo — viejo (old)	nuevo — nuevo (new)
feliz — feliz (happy)	triste — triste (sad)

old — viejo   pretty — bonita   sad — triste
big — grande   small — pequeño   happy — feliz
new — nuevo   dirty — sucio   ugly — feo
clean — limpio

Complete Book of Spanish • Grades 1-3   53

Page 54

Parts of Speech — Nombre _____

Abundant Adjectives

Circle the Spanish words you find in the word search. Then, write the English meanings next to the Spanish words at the bottom of the page.

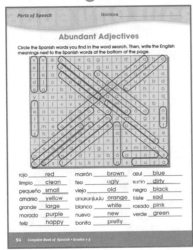

rojo — red   marrón — brown   azul — blue
limpio — clean   feo — ugly   sucio — dirty
pequeño — small   viejo — old   negro — black
amarillo — yellow   anaranjado — orange   triste — sad
grande — large   blanco — white   rosado — pink
morado — purple   nuevo — new   verde — green
feliz — happy   bonita — pretty

54   Complete Book of Spanish • Grades 1-3

Page 55

Parts of Speech — Nombre _____

Words to Describe

Descriptive adjectives are words that describe nouns. On this page and the next page, write the Spanish adjective that describes each picture.

Word Bank: feliz grande nuevo pequeño feo rica limpio sucia bonita triste viejo pobre alto bajo abierto cerrado

large — grande	new — nuevo	ugly — feo
happy — feliz	old — viejo	sad — triste
small — pequeño	clean — limpio	

Complete Book of Spanish • Grades 1-3   55

Page 56

Parts of Speech — Nombre _____

Words to Describe

Word Bank: feliz grande nuevo pequeño feo rica limpio sucia bonita triste viejo pobre alto bajo abierto cerrado

pretty — bonita	dirty — sucio	tall — alto
open — abierto	rich — rica	short — bajo
closed — cerrado	poor — pobre	

56   Complete Book of Spanish • Grades 1-3

Page 57

Parts of Speech — Nombre _____

Words to Describe

Write the Spanish words for the clue words in the crossword puzzle.

Across
3. poor
7. open
9. tall
11. clean
12. dirty
13. new

Down
1. ugly
2. closed
4. happy
5. pretty
6. large
8. old
10. sad

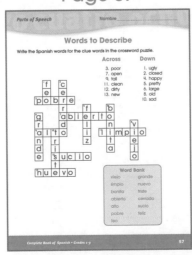

Word Bank: viejo grande limpio nuevo bonita triste abierto cerrado alto sucio pobre feliz feo

Complete Book of Spanish • Grades 1-3   57

Page 58

Parts of Speech — Nombre _____

Open and Close

Would you know what to do if your teacher told you to do something in Spanish? In each box, copy the Spanish word. Then, write the English word below it from the Word Bank.

Word Bank: sing sit down close glue open stop cut paint stand up draw

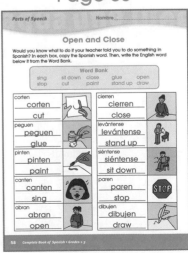

corten — corten (cut)	cierren — cierren (close)
peguen — peguen (glue)	levántense — levántense (stand up)
pinten — pinten (paint)	siéntense — siéntense (sit down)
canten — canten (sing)	paren — paren (stop)
abran — abran (open)	dibujen — dibujen (draw)

58   Complete Book of Spanish • Grades 1-3

Answer Key

Page 59

Write It Down

Write the Spanish word for each clue in the crossword puzzle.

Across
3. paint
4. open
7. stand up
8. sing
9. paste

Down
1. draw
2. sit down
5. close
6. stop

Crossword answers:
pinten, abran, levántense, canten, peguen

Word Bank
canten   cierren   levántense
paren   pinten   abran
siéntense peguen   dibujen

Page 61

Simon Says

Would you know what to do if your teacher asked you to do something in Spanish? On this page and the next page, copy the Spanish word. Then, write the English meaning below it.

Word Bank
sit down   glue   paint   close   run   listen
open   stand up cut   walk   write read

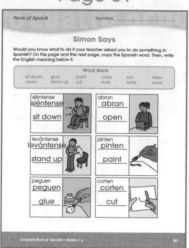

- siéntense — siéntense — sit down
- levántense — levántense — stand up
- peguen — peguen — glue
- abran — abran — open
- pinten — pinten — paint
- corten — corten — cut

Page 62

Simon Says

Word Bank
sit down   glue   paint   close   run   listen
open   stand up cut   walk   write read

- cierren — cierren — close
- caminen — caminen — walk
- escriban — escriban — write
- escuchen — escuchen — listen
- corran — corran — run
- lean — lean — read

Page 63

Search and Find

Circle the Spanish words you find in the word search. Write the English meanings at the bottom of the page next to the Spanish words from the puzzle.

Spanish Word	English	Spanish Word	English
corten	cut	corran	run
levántense	stand up	escriban	write
peguen	glue	abran	open
siéntense	sit down	escuchen	listen
caminen	walk	cierren	close
pinten	paint	lean	read

Page 64

Action Words

In each box, copy the Spanish action verbs. Then, write the English word below it.

Word Bank
to touch   to look at   to eat   to give
to drink   to speak   to clean to sleep

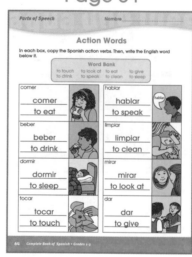

- comer — comer — to eat
- hablar — hablar — to speak
- beber — beber — to drink
- limpiar — limpiar — to clean
- dormir — dormir — to sleep
- mirar — mirar — to look at
- tocar — tocar — to touch
- dar — dar — to give

Page 65

Action Words

Write the Spanish words from the Word Bank that fit in these word blocks. Write the English meanings below the blocks.

Word Bank
mirar   limpiar   tocar   beber
hablar comer   dar   dormir

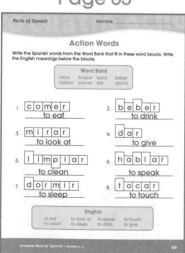

1. comer — to eat
2. beber — to drink
3. mirar — to look at
4. dar — to give
5. limpiar — to clean
6. hablar — to speak
7. dormir — to sleep
8. tocar — to touch

English
to eat   to look at   to speak   to touch
to clean   to sleep   to drink   to give

Page 66

First Sentences

Create original sentences in Spanish using the sentence starters and the verbs in the Word Bank. You may use one sentence starter more than once. Write the English meanings on the lines below the Spanish.

Word Bank
comer   beber   dormir   tocar
hablar limpiar mirar   dar

Sentence Starters
Me gusta _____.   (I like _____.)
No me gusta _____.   (I don't like _____.)
Quiero _____.   (I want _____.)
Necesito _____.   (I need _____.)

1. _____
2. _____
3. _____ Sentences Will Vary.
4. _____
5. _____

Page 67

Action Words

On this page and the next page, refer to the Word Bank to write the Spanish word that matches each picture.

Word Bank
comer   beber   mirar   tocar
hablar limpiar trabajar dar
estudiar dormir jugar   ir

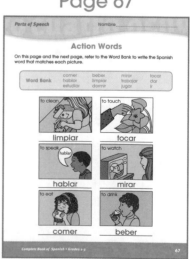

- to clean — limpiar
- to touch — tocar
- to speak — hablar
- to watch — mirar
- to eat — comer
- to drink — beber

Page 68

Action Words

Word Bank: comer, beber, mirar, tocar, hablar, limpiar, trabajar, dar, estudiar, dormir, jugar, ir

- to give — dar
- to sleep — dormir
- to go — ir
- to work — trabajar
- to study — estudiar
- to play — jugar

Page 69

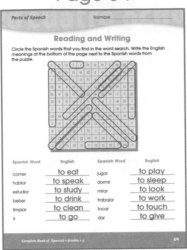

Reading and Writing

Circle the Spanish words that you find in the word search. Write the English meanings at the bottom of the page next to the Spanish words from the puzzle.

Spanish Word	English	Spanish Word	English
comer	to eat	jugar	to play
hablar	to speak	dormir	to sleep
estudiar	to study	mirar	to look
beber	to drink	trabajar	to work
limpiar	to clean	tocar	to touch
ir	to go	dar	to give

Page 70

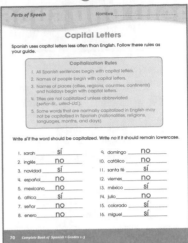

Capital Letters

Write *sí* if the word should be capitalized. Write *no* if it should remain lowercase.

1. sarah — sí
2. inglés — no
3. navidad — sí
4. español — no
5. mexicano — no
6. africa — sí
7. señor — no
8. enero — no
9. domingo — no
10. católico — no
11. santa fé — sí
12. viernes — no
13. méxico — sí
14. julio — no
15. colorado — sí
16. miguel — sí

Page 71

Categories

Read the list of words given. Write the words in the proper columns. If the word needs a capital letter, write it that way.

People	Places	Titles	Not Capitalized
María	Los Angeles	Uds.	inglés
Susana	San Diego	Sr.	señorita
Juan	España	Sra.	viernes
José	Cuba		ustedes
	San Antonio		septiembre
	Santa Fé		americano
	Océano Pacífico		español
	América del Norte		señora
	México		mexicano
			lunes
			católico
			señor

Page 75

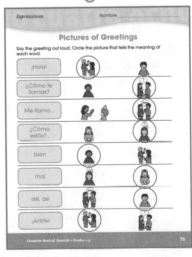

Pictures of Greetings

Say the greeting out loud. Circle the picture that tells the meaning of each word.

¡Hola! / ¿Cómo te llamas? / Me llamo... / ¿Cómo estás?.. / bien / mal / así, así / ¡Adiós!

Page 76

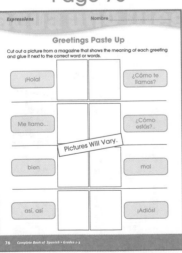

Greetings Paste Up

Cut out a picture from a magazine that shows the meaning of each greeting and glue it next to the correct word or words.

¡Hola! / ¿Cómo te llamas? / Me llamo... / ¿Cómo estás?.. / bien / mal / así, así / ¡Adiós!

Pictures Will Vary.

Page 78

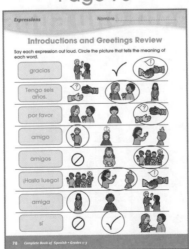

Introductions and Greetings Review

Say each expression out loud. Circle the picture that tells the meaning of each word.

gracias / Tengo seis años. / por favor / amigo / amigos / ¡Hasta luego! / amiga / sí

Page 79

What's Your Name?

Word Bank: I'm so-so. / What's your name? / I'm well/fine. / I'm ___ years old. / I'm not doing well. / My name is ___. / I'm not well. / How are you? / How old are you?

Refer to the Word Bank to translate the Spanish questions and answers into English.

1. ¿Cómo te llamas? **What is your name?**
   Me llamo **My name is ___.**
2. ¿Cómo estás? **How are you?**
   Estoy bien/mal/así así. **I'm fine. I'm not well. I'm so-so.**
3. ¿Cuántos años tienes? **How old are you?**
   Tengo ___ años. **I am ___ years old.**

Word Bank: hello / please / friend / yes / no / thank you / goodbye / See you later!

Write the English meaning after the Spanish word.

4. hola — hello
5. amigo, amiga — friend (m/f)
6. sí — yes
7. no — no
8. por favor — please
9. gracias — thank you
10. ¡Hasta luego! — See you later!
11. adiós — goodbye

Answer Key

Page 80

Expressions   Nombre_____

Word Blocks

Write the Spanish words from the Word Bank that fit in the word blocks. Don't forget the punctuation. Write the English meanings below the blocks.

1. h o l a — hello
2. p o r   f a v o r — please
3. n o — no
4. ¡H a s t a   l u e g o! — See you later!
5. ¿C ó m o   e s t á s? — How are you?
6. ¿C ó m o   t e   l l a m a s? — What is your name?
7. a d i ó s — goodbye
8. E s t o y   b i e n. — I am fine.

Spanish Word Bank
por favor, adiós, Estoy bien., hola, ¡Hasta luego!, ¿Cómo te llamas?, no, ¿Cómo estás?

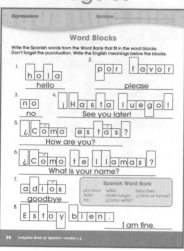

Page 81

Expressions   Nombre_____

Greetings

Use the Word Bank to write the English meaning of the Spanish words and phrases.

1. señor — Mr.
2. señora — Mrs.
3. señorita — Miss
4. maestro — teacher (male)
5. maestra — teacher (female)
6. ¡Buenos días! — Good morning!
7. ¡Buenas tardes! — Good afternoon!
8. ¡Buenas noches! — Good night!
9. Vamos a contar. — Let's count.

Word Bank
Mr., Good night!, Good morning!, Good afternoon!, teacher (female), teacher (male), Miss, Let's count.

Draw a picture to show the time of day that you use each expression.

Pictures Will Vary.

¡Buenos días! | ¡Buenas tardes! | ¡Buenas noches!

Page 82

Expressions   Nombre_____

Spanish Greetings

Write the Spanish word for each clue in the crossword puzzle.

Across
1. bad
4. good
7. teacher (male)
9. friend (female)
10. Mr.
11. Miss

Down
2. friend (male)
3. hello
5. thank you
6. goodbye
7. teacher (female)
8. Mrs.

Word Bank
amiga, mal, señora, señor, maestra, bien, adiós, hola, señorita, gracias, amigo, maestra

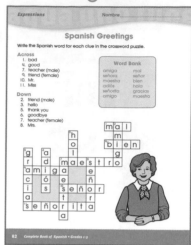

Page 83

Expressions   Nombre_____

Greetings

Refer to the Word Bank to translate the Spanish greetings, questions, and answers.

¡Buenos días! — Good morning!
¡Buenas tardes! — Good afternoon!
¡Buenas noches! — Good night!
¿Cómo estás? — How are you?
bien, gracias — fine, thank you
mal — not well
así así — ok/so-so
¿Cómo te llamas? — What is your name?
Me llamo — My name is
¿Cuántos años tienes? — How old are you?
Tengo ___ años. — I am ___ years old.
adiós — goodbye   hola — hello

Word Bank
goodbye, Good morning!, I am ___ years old., fine, thank you, Good afternoon!, hello, How old are you?, How are you?, What is your name?, My name is ___., not well, ok/so-so, Good night!

Word Bank
teacher (m/f), Miss, no, Mr., friend (m/f), please, Mrs., yes

Refer to the Word Bank to translate the Spanish vocabulary.

amigo/amiga — friend (m/f)
sí — yes   no — no   por favor — please
señor — Mr.   señora — Mrs.
maestro/maestra — teacher (m/f)
señorita — Miss

Page 84

Expressions   Nombre_____

Find the Words

Circle the Spanish words that you find in the word search. Then, write the English meanings at the bottom of the page next to the Spanish words from the puzzle.

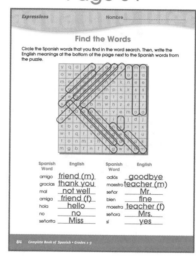

Spanish Word	English	Spanish Word	English
amigo	friend (m)	adiós	goodbye
gracias	thank you	maestro	teacher (m)
mal	not well	señor	Mr.
amiga	friend (f)	bien	fine
hola	hello	maestra	teacher (f)
no	no	señora	Mrs.
señorita	Miss	sí	yes

Page 87

Days and Months   Nombre_____

Seven Days

Copy the Spanish words for the days of the week. In Spanish-speaking countries, lunes is the first day of the week.

Monday	lunes	lunes
Tuesday	martes	martes
Wednesday	miércoles	miércoles
Thursday	jueves	jueves
Friday	viernes	viernes
Saturday	sábado	sábado
Sunday	domingo	domingo

Draw a line to match the Spanish and English days of the week.

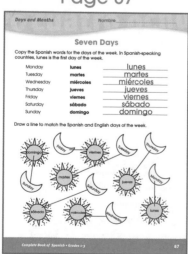

Page 88

Days and Months   Nombre_____

Puzzle of the Week

Write the Spanish words in the puzzle.

Across
2. Thursday
7. Wednesday

Down
1. Monday
3. Saturday
4. Friday
5. Sunday
6. Tuesday

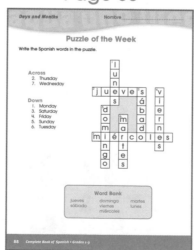

Word Bank
jueves, domingo, martes, sábado, viernes, lunes, miércoles

Page 90

Days and Months   Nombre_____

Yesterday and Today

Write the Spanish words for the days of the week. Remember, in Spanish-speaking countries, Monday is the first day of the week.

Word Bank
miércoles, lunes, martes, viernes, domingo, jueves, sábado

Monday	lunes
Tuesday	martes
Wednesday	miércoles
Thursday	jueves
Friday	viernes
Saturday	sábado
Sunday	domingo

If today is Monday, yesterday was Sunday. Complete the following chart by identifying the missing days in Spanish.

ayer (yesterday)	hoy (today)	mañana (tomorrow)
martes	miércoles	jueves
lunes	martes	miércoles
jueves	viernes	sábado
sábado	domingo	lunes
miércoles	jueves	viernes
domingo	lunes	martes
viernes	sábado	domingo

Page 91

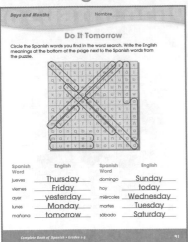

Page 92

Page 93

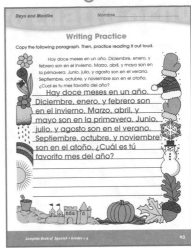

Page 94

Page 97

Page 98

Page 99

Page 100

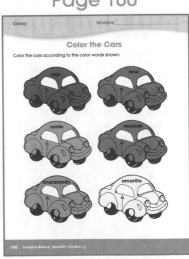

Answer Key

Page 101

Page 102

Page 103

Page 104

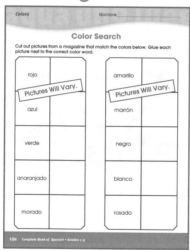

Page 105

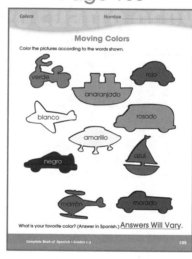

Page 106

Page 107

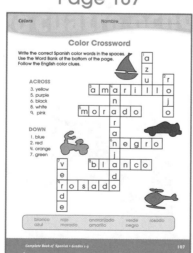

Page 108

Answer Key

Page 109

Colorful Flowers

Color the flowers according to the Spanish color words shown below.

Page 110

Color Find

Circle the Spanish color words that you find in the word search. Then, write the English meaning of each word.

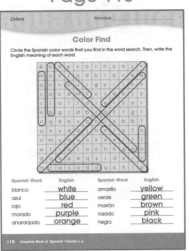

Spanish Word	English	Spanish Word	English
blanco	white	amarillo	yellow
azul	blue	verde	green
rojo	red	marrón	brown
morado	purple	rosado	pink
anaranjado	orange	negro	black

Page 111

Draw and Color

In each box, write the Spanish color word. Use the Word Bank below to help you. Then, draw and color a picture of something that is that color.

red is __rojo__   orange is __anaranjado__   brown is __marrón__

Pictures Will Vary.

blue is __azul__   purple is __morado__   black is __negro__

green is __verde__   yellow is __amarillo__   pink is __rosado__

Which Spanish color from the Word Bank is not used above? __blanco__

Word Bank

blanco	rojo	amarillo	rosado
azul	morado	verde	negro
	anaranjado	marrón	

Page 112

Butterfly Garden

Color the butterfly garden as indicated in Spanish.

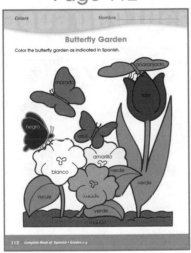

Page 113

Across the Spectrum

Write the Spanish for each clue word in the crossword puzzle.

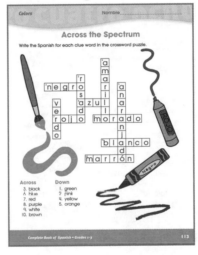

Across
3. black
6. blue
7. red
8. purple
9. white
10. brown

Down
1. green
2. pink
4. yellow
5. orange

Page 117

My Meal

Draw or cut out pictures of food and glue them on the plate to make a meal. Which food is your favorite?

Mi comida

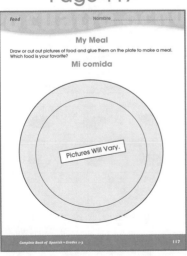

Pictures Will Vary.

Page 118

Food Meanings

Say each word out loud. Circle the picture that shows the meaning of each word.

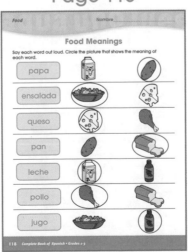

papa

ensalada

queso

pan

leche

pollo

jugo

Page 119

Mixed-Up Food

Draw a line from the word to the food picture.

papa

ensalada

queso

pan

leche

jugo

pollo

Answer Key

Page 120

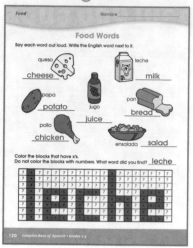

Page 121

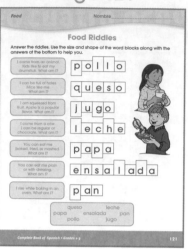

Page 122

Page 123

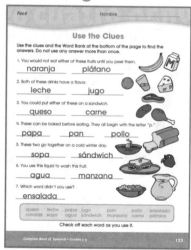

Page 124

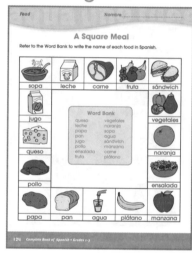

Page 125

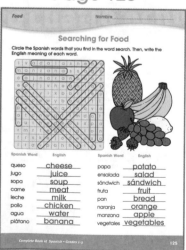

Page 126

Page 127

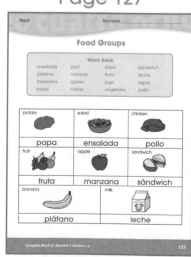

Page 128

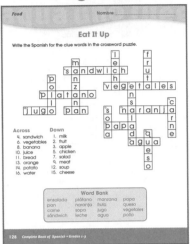

Food — Nombre _____

Eat It Up

Write the Spanish for the clue words in the crossword puzzle.

Across
4. sandwich
6. vegetables
8. banana
10. juice
11. bread
13. orange
14. potato
16. water

Down
1. milk
2. fruit
3. apple
5. chicken
7. salad
9. meat
12. soup
15. cheese

Word Bank

ensalada	plátano	manzana	papa
pan	naranja	fruta	queso
carne	sopa	jugo	vegetales
sándwich	leche	agua	pollo

128 Complete Book of Spanish • Grades 1-3

Page 131

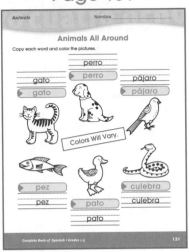

Animals — Nombre _____

Animals All Around

Copy each word and color the pictures.

perro
gato — perro — pájaro
gato — pájaro
Colors Will Vary.
pez
pez — pato — culebra
pato — culebra

131 Complete Book of Spanish • Grades 1-3

Page 132

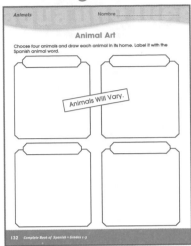

Animals — Nombre _____

Animal Art

Choose four animals and draw each animal in its home. Label it with the Spanish animal word.

Animals Will Vary.

132 Complete Book of Spanish • Grades 1-3

Page 133

Animals — Nombre _____

Animal Crossword

Use the picture clues to complete the puzzle. Choose from the Spanish words at the bottom of the page. One is done for you.

culebra
pájaro
oso
pato
pez

| oso | perro | pájaro |
| pez | pato | culebra |

133 Complete Book of Spanish • Grades 1-3

Page 134

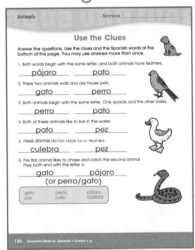

Animals — Nombre _____

Use the Clues

Answer the questions. Use the clues and the Spanish words at the bottom of the page. You may use answers more than once.

1. Both words begin with the same letter, and both animals have feathers.
   pájaro   pato
2. These two animals walk and are house pets.
   gato   perro
3. Both animals begin with the same letter. One quacks and the other barks.
   perro   pato
4. Both of these animals like to live in the water.
   pato   pez
5. These animals do not have fur or feathers.
   culebra   pez
6. The first animal likes to chase and catch the second animal. They both end with the letter o.
   gato   pájaro
   (or perro/gato)

| gato | perro | pájaro |
| pez | pato | culebra |

134 Complete Book of Spanish • Grades 1-3

Page 135

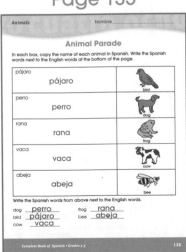

Animals — Nombre _____

Animal Parade

In each box, copy the name of each animal in Spanish. Write the Spanish words next to the English words at the bottom of the page.

pájaro	pájaro	bird
perro	perro	dog
rana	rana	frog
vaca	vaca	cow
abeja	abeja	bee

Write the Spanish words from above next to the English words.

dog perro   frog rana
bird pájaro   bee abeja
cow vaca

135 Complete Book of Spanish • Grades 1-3

Page 136

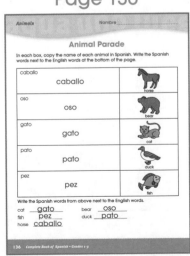

Animals — Nombre _____

Animal Parade

In each box, copy the name of each animal in Spanish. Write the Spanish words next to the English words at the bottom of the page.

caballo	caballo	horse
oso	oso	bear
gato	gato	cat
pato	pato	duck
pez	pez	fish

Write the Spanish words from above next to the English words.

cat gato   bear oso
fish pez   duck pato
horse caballo

136 Complete Book of Spanish • Grades 1-3

Page 137

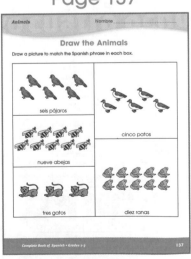

Animals — Nombre _____

Draw the Animals

Draw a picture to match the Spanish phrase in each box.

seis pájaros   cinco patos
nueve abejas
tres gatos   diez ranas

137 Complete Book of Spanish • Grades 1-3

Answer Key

Page 138

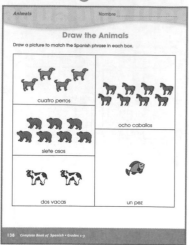

Page 140

Page 141

Page 145

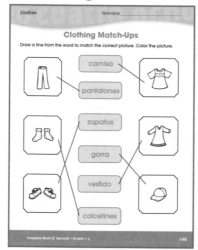

Page 146

Page 147

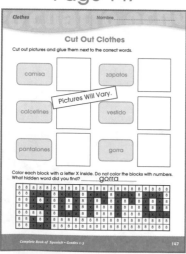

Page 148

Page 149

Answer Key

Page 150

Remember These?

Fill in the blanks with the missing letters. Use the Spanish clothing words at the bottom to help you.

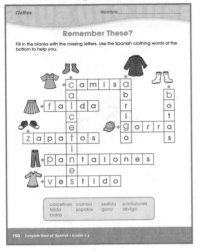

Word bank:
calcetines camisa vestido pantalones
falda zapatos gorra abrigo

Page 151

What Belongs?

Circle the item that does not belong with the other two. Write the name in Spanish below its picture.

gorra

guantes

pantalones

Page 152

What Belongs?

Circle the two items that are alike. Say the item in Spanish that is not like the other two. Color the pictures.

Page 153

Clothes Closet

On this page and the next page, refer to the Word Bank and write the Spanish word for each item of clothing pictured.

Word Bank
vestido cinturón pantalones
sombrero pantalones cortos zapatos
guantes botas chaqueta
calcetines falda camisa

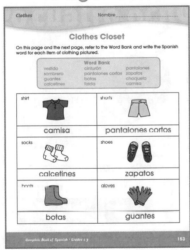

shirt	shorts
camisa	pantalones cortos
socks	shoes
calcetines	zapatos
boots	gloves
botas	guantes

Page 154

Clothes Closet

Word Bank
vestido cinturón pantalones
sombrero pantalones cortos zapatos
guantes botas chaqueta
calcetines falda camisa

pants	hat
pantalones	sombrero
skirt	belt
falda	cinturón
dress	jacket
vestido	chaqueta

Page 155

Dressing Up

Write the Spanish word for each clue in the crossword puzzle.

Across
1. shoes   8. gloves
4. socks   9. hat
7. dress   10. shirt

Down
2. pants   5. belt
3. skirt   6. boots
4. jacket

Word Bank
cinturón botas camisa
guantes calcetines sombrero
chaqueta falda zapatos
pantalones vestido

Page 156

Colorful Clothing

Copy each sentence in Spanish on the first line. Write the English meaning on the second line.

1. El vestido es rojo. — El vestido es rojo. / The dress is red.
2. La camisa es marrón. — La camisa es marrón. / The shirt is brown.
3. El sombrero es morado. — El sombrero es morado. / The hat is purple.
4. La falda es verde. — La falda es verde. / The skirt is green.
5. El vestido es rosado. — El vestido es rosado. / The dress is pink.
6. La chaqueta es azul. — La chaqueta es azul. / The jacket is blue.
7. Los calcetines son amarillos. — Los calcetines son amarillos. / The socks are yellow.
8. El cinturón es anaranjado. — El cinturón es anaranjado. / The belt is orange.
9. Las botas son blancas. — Las botas son blancas. / The boots are white.

Page 157

Matching Clothes

Underneath each picture, write the English word that matches the Spanish and the pictures. Write the Spanish words next to the English words at the bottom of the page.

falda	zapatos
skirt	shoes
abrigo	calcetines
coat	socks
guantes	pantalones
gloves	pants
gorra	sandalias
cap	sandals

1. skirt __falda__
2. socks __calcetines__
3. coat __abrigo__
4. sandals __sandalias__
5. cap __gorra__
6. pants __pantalones__
7. gloves __guantes__
8. shoes __zapatos__

Answer Key

Page 158

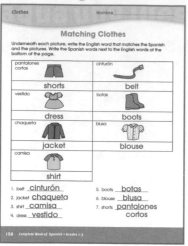

Matching Clothes

Underneath each picture, write the English word that matches the Spanish and the pictures. Write the Spanish words next to the English words at the bottom of the page.

pantalones cortos	cinturón
shorts	belt
vestido	botas
dress	boots
chaqueta	blusa
jacket	blouse
camisa	
shirt	

1. belt **cinturón**
2. jacket **chaqueta**
3. shirt **camisa**
4. dress **vestido**
5. boots **botas**
6. blouse **blusa**
7. shorts **pantalones cortos**

158 Complete Book of Spanish • Grades 1-3

Page 159

Clothes Closet

Circle the Spanish words that you find in the puzzle. Write the English meanings at the bottom of the page next to the Spanish words from the puzzle.

Spanish Word	English	Spanish Word	English
abrigo	coat	sandalias	sandals
guantes	gloves	calcetines	socks
blusa	blouse	falda	skirt
chaqueta	jacket	vestido	dress
pantalones	pants	camisa	shirt
botas	boots	gorra	cap
cinturón	belt	zapatos	shoes

Complete Book of Spanish • Grades 1-3 159

Page 162

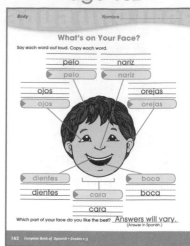

What's on Your Face?

Say each word out loud. Copy each word.

pelo — pelo
nariz — nariz
ojos — ojos
orejas — orejas
dientes — dientes
boca — boca
cara — cara

Which part of your face do you like the best? **Answers will vary.**
(Answer in Spanish.)

162 Complete Book of Spanish • Grades 1-3

Page 163

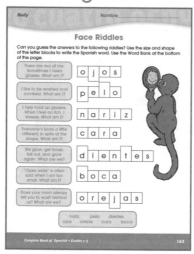

Face Riddles

Can you guess the answers to the following riddles? Use the size and shape of the letter blocks to write the Spanish word. Use the Word Bank at the bottom of the page.

There are two of me. Sometimes I need glasses. What am I? → **ojos**

I like to be washed and combed. What am I? → **pelo**

I help hold up glasses. When I feel an itch, I sneeze. What am I? → **nariz**

Everyone's looks a little different, in spite of the shape. What am I? → **cara**

We grow, get loose, fall out, and grow again. What are we? → **dientes**

"Open wide" is often said when I am too small. What am I? → **boca**

Does your mom always tell you to wash behind us? What are we? → **orejas**

Word Bank: nariz pelo dientes ojos orejas cara boca

Complete Book of Spanish • Grades 1-3 163

Page 164

A Blank Face

Fill in the blanks with the missing letters. Use the Spanish words below to help you.

dientes nariz boca pelo orejas

Word Bank: nariz pelo dientes ojos orejas cara boca

Which word didn't you use? **cara**

Color each block that has a letter k inside. Do not color the blocks with numbers. What hidden word did you find? **boca**

164 Complete Book of Spanish • Grades 1-3

Page 165

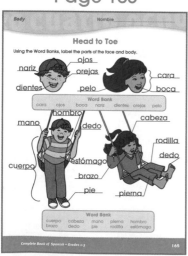

Head to Toe

Using the Word Banks, label the parts of the face and body.

nariz ojos orejas cara dientes pelo boca

Word Bank: cara ojos boca nariz dientes orejas pelo

hombro cabeza mano dedo rodilla cuerpo estómago brazo pie pierna dedo

Word Bank: cuerpo cabeza mano pierna hombro brazo dedo pie rodilla estómago

Complete Book of Spanish • Grades 1-3 165

Page 166

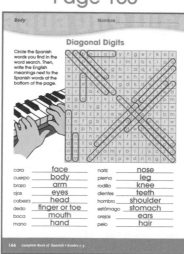

Diagonal Digits

Circle the Spanish words you find in the word search. Then, write the English meanings next to the Spanish words at the bottom of the page.

cara	face	nariz	nose
cuerpo	body	pierna	leg
brazo	arm	rodilla	knee
ojos	eyes	dientes	teeth
cabeza	head	hombro	shoulder
dedo	finger or toe	estómago	stomach
boca	mouth	orejas	ears
mano	hand	pelo	hair

166 Complete Book of Spanish • Grades 1-3

Page 167

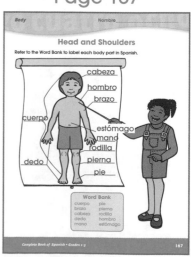

Head and Shoulders

Refer to the Word Bank to label each body part in Spanish.

cabeza hombro brazo cuerpo estómago mano rodilla dedo pierna pie

Word Bank: cuerpo brazo cabeza dedo mano pie pierna rodilla hombro estómago

Complete Book of Spanish • Grades 1-3 167

Page 168

Body   Nombre _____

Knees and Toes

Write the Spanish words for the clues in the crossword puzzle.

Word Bank
cuerpo   cabeza   mano   pierna   hombro
brazo   dedo   pie   rodilla   estómago

Across
2. foot
3. body
5. knee
6. head
7. shoulder
9. hand

Down
1. finger or toe
2. leg
4. stomach
8. arm

Page 169

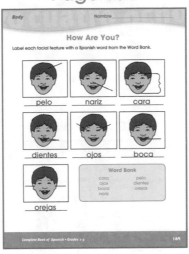

Body   Nombre _____

How Are You?

Label each facial feature with a Spanish word from the Word Bank.

pelo   nariz   cara

dientes   ojos   boca

orejas

Word Bank
cara   pelo
ojos   dientes
boca   orejas
nariz

Page 170

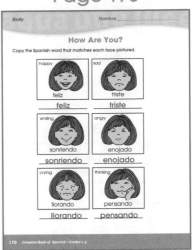

Body   Nombre _____

How Are You?

Copy the Spanish word that matches each face pictured.

happy — feliz — feliz
sad — triste — triste
smiling — sonriendo — sonriendo
angry — enojada — enojado
crying — llorando — llorando
thinking — pensando — pensando

Page 171

Body   Nombre _____

Happy or Sad?

Write the Spanish for the clue words in the crossword puzzle.

Across
1. sad
2. eyes
3. thinking
5. face
10. smiling
11. crying

Down
4. angry
6. teeth
7. ears
8. mouth
9. hair

Word Bank
llorando   orejas   sonriendo   ojos
pelo   pensando   triste   cara
dientes   boca   enojado

Page 175

Family   Nombre _____

My Family

Draw a picture of your family. Color your picture.

Mi familia

Pictures Will Vary.

Write the correct Spanish word next to each person in your picture above.

padre   abuelo   hermana
hermano   madre   abuela

Page 176

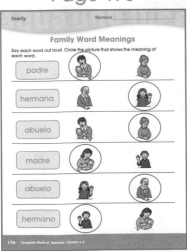

Family   Nombre _____

Family Word Meanings

Say each word out loud. Circle the picture that shows the meaning of each word.

padre
hermana
abuela
madre
abuelo
hermano

Page 177

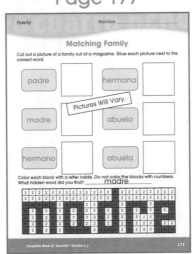

Family   Nombre _____

Matching Family

Cut out a picture of a family out of a magazine. Glue each picture next to the correct word.

padre   hermana
madre   abuelo
hermano   abuela

Pictures Will Vary.

Color each block with a letter inside. Do not color the blocks with numbers. What hidden word did you find? madre

Page 178

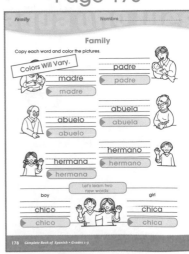

Family   Nombre _____

Family

Copy each word and color the pictures.

Colors Will Vary.

madre — padre — padre
madre
abuelo — abuela — abuela
hermano — hermana — hermano
hermana

Let's learn two new words:
boy — chico — chico
girl — chica — chica

Page 179

Family Crossword

Use the Spanish words at the bottom of the page to fill in your answers.

Crossword answers:
- ¹h e r m a n a
- ³p a d r e
- ⁵m a d r e
- ⁶c h i c a
- ⁷c h i c o
- (down) ²a b u e l a, ³a b u e l o

ACROSS
1. sister
4. father
5. mother
6. girl
7. boy

DOWN
1. brother
2. grandmother
3. grandfather

Word bank:
padre, chico, abuelo, hermano, madre, chica, abuela, hermana

Complete Book of Spanish • Grades 1-3 179

Page 180

Listen Well

Say each word out loud. Circle the picture for each Spanish word.

padre
abuelo
hermana
chica
abuela
madre
hermano
chico

180 *Complete Book of Spanish • Grades 1-3*

Page 181

Family Ties

In each box, copy the Spanish word for family members.

la familia	el padre
la familia — family	el padre — father
la madre	el hijo
la madre — mother	el hijo — son
la hija	los primos
la hija — daughter	los primos — cousins

Write the Spanish words from above next to the English words.

family **la familia**   mother **la madre**
cousins **los primos**   daughter **la hija**
father **el padre**   son **el hijo**

Complete Book of Spanish • Grades 1-3 181

Page 182

Family Ties

In each box, copy the Spanish word for family members.

el hermano	la hermana
el hermano — brother	la hermana — sister
el tío	la tía
el tío — uncle	la tía — aunt
el abuelo	la abuela
el abuelo — grandfather	la abuela — grandmother

Write the Spanish words from above next to the English words.

sister **la hermana**   uncle **el tío**
grandfather **el abuelo**   brother **el hermano**
grandmother **la abuela**   aunt **la tía**

182 *Complete Book of Spanish • Grades 1-3*

Page 183

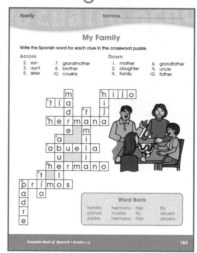

My Family

Write the Spanish word for each clue in the crossword puzzle.

Across
2. son
3. aunt
5. sister
7. grandmother
8. brother
10. cousins

Down
1. mother
2. daughter
4. family
6. grandfather
9. uncle
10. father

Crossword answers include: hijo, tía, hermana, abuela, hermano, primos, madre, familia

Word Bank
familia, primos, padre, hermano, madre, hermana, hijo, tío, hija, tía, abuelo, abuela

Complete Book of Spanish • Grades 1-3 183